Anglican Liturgical Inculturation in Africa

The Kanamai Statement

with Introduction, Papers from Kanamai and a first Response

edited by David Gitari

Bishop of Kirinyaga, Church of the Province of Kenya

Convenor of the Kanamai Consultation, 31 May-4 June 1993

Chapter 3 is also available as a separate booklet, *African Culture and Anglican Liturgy*, from Grove Books Ltd.

THE ALCUIN CLUB and the GROUP FOR RENEWAL OF WORSHIP (GROW)

The Alcuin Club, which exists to promote the study of Christian liturgy in general and of Anglican liturgy in particular, traditionally published a single volume annually for its members. This ceased in 1986 but resumed in 1992. Similarly, GROW was responsible from 1975 to 1986 for the quarterly 'Grove Liturgical Studies'. Since the beginning of 1987 the two have sponsored a Joint Editorial Board to produce quarterly 'Joint Liturgical Studies', details of which are to be found at the end of this Study.

First Impression June 1994

ISSN 0951-2667

ISBN 1 85174 270 0

CONTENTS

THE CONTRIBUTORS

Colin Buchanan is an Assistant Bishop in the diocese of Rochester, Church of England.

Elisha Mbonigaba is lecturer in liturgy at Bishop Tucker Theological College, Mulkono, Church of Uganda.

Solomon Amusan is lecturer in liturgy at Vining College of Theology, Province of Nigeria.

Introduction

by Bishop David Gitari
Bishop of Kirinyaga, Church of the Province of Kenya
Convenor of the Kanamai Consultation

The Kanamai Consultation is now history, and this Study is being published just a year after the 43 of us met at Kanamai to work together on principles of the inculturation of Anglican liturgy in Africa. The twelve months have themselves been a momentous time for Africa; for instance, you will find in the Introduction to the actual Statement which I wrote a year ago that we rejoiced at Kanamai to hear of the election of a president of Burundi—but since then he has been murdered along with the then president of Rwanda, both countries have broken into Civil War, and our own friends from those countries who were with us at Kanamai have been swept into the suffering and agonies of those terrible conflicts. At Kanamai too we could not but be conscious of the continued harassment of the Christian Church in Southern Sudan, as the Province of Sudan could only be represented by a clergyman in exile. On the other hand, we have very good news as I write this, as the whole of Africa rejoices together at the ending of the rule of apartheid in South Africa, and the coming of freedom for all races there. And we rejoice too at the confidence placed in our West African representative, Bishop Robert Okine from Ghana, as he has now become Archbishop of the Province of West Africa.

This Study is intended to take the work done at Kanamai a further stage into African and world consciousness. The Study includes the original Statement, which was published by Grove Books Ltd. in England in July 1993, and was circulated round the world as an inset to *News of Liturgy* in that same month (and is still available as a sixteen-page pamphlet). However, the provision by the Joint Editorial Board of the Alcuin Club and the Group for Renewal of Worship for this larger volume to be published does enable other material relating to the Kanamai Consultation to gain wider circulation. I would rejoice especially if it could be known all round Africa.

There is a complex but interesting history that lay behind the Kanamai Consultation, and I am glad of the chance to put it into a larger historical context. Once upon a time (and it feels a long time ago now) the metropolitans of the Anglican Provinces in Africa asked Leslie Brown, then Archbishop of Uganda, to draft 'A Liturgy for Africa'. It was duly published in 1964.[1] But it had little or nothing that was truly African about it, and, although it had some influence on the East African Union Liturgy (devised in 1966 for a projected union of Churches in Kenya and Tanzania), and through that liturgy upon the Tanzanian

[1] An introduction to *A Liturgy for Africa*, along with its text, is provided in Colin Buchanan (ed.) *Modern Anglican Liturgies 1958-1968* (Oxford, 1968) pp.48-69, and other discussion of it is in Leslie Brown, *Relevant Liturgy* (SPCK, 1965).

Liturgy (1973) also, yet in principle the actual text of the eucharistic liturgy was not in itself such as to enable anyone who picked it up in any other part of the world to see that its provenance and intended clientele were the Anglican Provinces of Africa.

Elisha Mbonigaba in his paper in this Study recalls Lambeth Conference findings of 1978 and 1988, though his quotation of documents of Vatican II would seem to be more far-reaching than the Lambeth Statements. The origins of a concern for indigenization and thus for the Kanamai Consultation would appear to lie more in the coming together of the International Anglican Liturgical Consultations (IALCs)(which began in 1985), and in the concerns of the Council of Anglican Provinces in Africa (CAPA), under whose aegis the Kanamai Consultation met.

The first meeting of IALC in Boston in 1985 had only fifteen participants, of whom none was black and practically none was African. The subject was admission to communion.[1] The second IALC met in Northern Italy in 1987, had more participants, including two notable Africans who were both later at Kanamai, Elisha Mbonigaba of Uganda and Themba Vundla of Southern Africa. The subject was the role of the laity in worship, but such a broad target enabled Elisha Mbonigaba to give a most penetrating paper on 'Indigenization of the Liturgy'.[1] There is reason to think this lit a fuse, for the following year the Lambeth Conference gave considerable space to the issue in its Statement and also unanimously passed plenary resolutions as follows:

RESOLUTION 22: CHRIST AND CULTURE

This Conference:

(a) Recognizes that culture is the context in which people find their identity.

(b) Affirms that God's love extends to people of every culture and that the Gospel judges every culture according to the Gospel's own criteria of truth, challenging some aspects of culture while endorsing and transforming others for the benefit of the Church and society.

(c) Urges the Church everywhere to work at expressing the unchanging Gospel of Christ in words, actions, names, customs, liturgies, which communicate relevantly in each contemporary society.

RESOLUTION 47: LITURGICAL FREEDOM

This Conference resolves that each Province should be free, subject to essential universal norms of worship and to a valuing of traditional liturgical

---

[1] The Boston statement was published as 'Children and Communion' in pamphlet form immediately after the Consultation, and was then incorporated in a fuller set of Boston papers published as: Colin Buchanan (ed.) *Nurturing Children in Communion* (Grove Liturgical Study no. 44, Grove Books Ltd, Bramcote, 1985). This Study is currently out of print and a new updated collection of 'Boston' material is expected from the USA during 1994.

[2] Most of the 'Brixen' papers, including Elisha Mbonigaba's, were published in Thomas Talley (ed.), *A Kingdom of Priests: Liturgical Formation of the People of God* (Alcuin/GROW Joint Liturgical Study no. 5, Grove Books Ltd., Bramcote, 1988).

materials, to seek that expression of worship which is appropriate to its Christian people in their cultural context.[1]

In passing I should mention here another relevant publication of that year—Phillip Tovey, *Inculturation: The Eucharist in Africa.*[2] Whilst this was an independent piece of work (from one who had lectured in Uganda), it highlighted many principles important to the furtherance of inculturation in Africa, and included as an appendix part of the first edition of the experimental eucharistic rite from my own Church of the Province of Kenya.

The next stage was the third IALC, which met at York in 1989. This time the theme of the whole Consultation was 'Inculturation of the Liturgy', and the attendance had risen to over thirty, including representatives from four Provinces in Africa. Themba Vundla had returned, and Solomon Amusan, who was in Birmingham doing a doctoral thesis on inculturation of liturgy in his own country, Nigeria, joined the IALC for the first time. The Consultation took as its text the Lambeth 1988 Resolution quoted above, and, in faithfulness to its terms, produced (among other findings) a manifesto on inculturation, entitled 'Down to Earth Worship'.[3] Then the papers of the Consultation were drawn together and edited into a Study in this series, and published in 1990.[4] That Study in turn proved to be part of the fuelling of the Kanamai Consultation.

The fourth IALC met in Toronto in 1991, and now there were over sixty participants. I found myself in the company of international liturgists for the first time, as, because I chair the Kenyan Liturgical Committee which had published two successive editions of a somewhat more African eucharist, I was asked to participate. There were seven African representatives, including Bishop Robert Okine from Ghana, Bishop Gideon Olajide from Nigeria, Bishop Yoram Bamunoha from Uganda, and Themba Vundla and Solomon Amusan who had been present in 1989. Elisha Mbonigaba from Uganda, as he mentions in his own paper was at a different conference in Harare at the same time. The seven of us were glad to go along with the initiation theme of the Consultation.[5] However, we knew we also had some distinct African agenda which had to be

---

[1] The Resolutions of the 1988 Lambeth Conference were published in *The Truth Shall Make You Free: The Lambeth Conference 1988: The Reports, Resolutions & Pastoral Letters from the Bishops* (ACC, 1989), and the whole set of Lambeth Statements is contained in the same report. For a commentary on the treatment of liturgy at the Conference see Colin Buchanan (ed.). *Lambeth and Liturgy 1988* (Grove Worship Series no. 106, Grove Books Ltd., Bramcote, 1989).

[2] This Study was Alcuin/GROW Joint Liturgical Study no. 7 (Grove Books Ltd., Bramcote, 1988).

[3] There exists a slim pamphlet, *Findings of the Third IALC, York 1989* (Grove Books Ltd., Bramcote, 1989) in which 'Down to Earth Worship' is a major component. But it is also contained in the Study mentioned in note 4 below this.

[4] These are contained in David Holeton (ed.), *Liturgical Inculturation in the Anglican Communion* (Alcuin/GROW Joint Liturgical Study no. 15, Grove Books Ltd., Bramcote, 1990).

[5] The Toronto Statement ('Walk in Newness of Life') was published in David Holeton (ed.), *Christian Initiation in the Anglican Communion* (Grove Worship Series no. 118, Grove Books, Bramcote, 1991). It too has been re-published with a set of essays as David Holeton (ed.), *Growing in Newness of Life* (Anglican Book Centre, Toronto, 1993).

addressed and, meeting with each other, laid a tentative plan for an African Consultation. Later, I was asked by CAPA to convene a Consultation, and it was this request which led to the gathering at Kanamai.

This Study includes the actual Kanamai Statement with the Introduction I wrote for its original publication (it was then a 16-page document entitled *African Culture and Anglican Liturgy*), and that occupies pages 33 to 48 below. Leading into it are edited versions of the two opening papers read at Kanamai on 'Liturgical Inculturation' by Colin Buchanan and Elisha Mbonigaba—papers which neatly complement each other, as the first of them accounts for the (uninculturated) ways Anglican liturgy developed in Africa in the past, and the second of them calls for a complete about-turn from those ways and the adoption of truly indigenized liturgy in all parts of the continent.

The last contribution to this Study is a short paper by Solomon Amusan from Nigeria. It was a matter for grief that, largely for administrative reasons, the Province of Nigeria, alone of the main African Provinces, was unable to send representatives to Kanamai. It is all the more appropriate that a well-known liturgical scholar from Nigeria, one who has attended the last two IALCs, should now give the first considered response to the Kanamai Statement. The truest set of responses will come in the actual changes to liturgy the various African Provinces make as they discover liturgical principles—including those of inculturation—which will enable them to steer a creative course into their particular liturgical futures. My own hope would be that, by the time the next African Consultation occurs in 1996, there will be much more first-hand evidence of the principles of the Kanamai Statement being worked out in every Province.

Meanwhile the rest of the Anglican world has not been idle. An interim IALC met at Untermarchtal in South Germany two months after Kanamai, and did preparatory work on ways of revising the eucharist, work that was in preparation for the next (i.e. the fifth) full IALC at Dublin in August 1995.[1] This Consultation was avowedly 'interim', as no funds were available (as we hope they will be in Dublin) to pay for participants from the financially poorer parts of the Anglican Communion. Only three people who were at Kanamai re-appeared at Untermarchtal (Colin Buchanan, Paul Gibson, and Themba Vundla). Thus, from an African perspective, that Consultation was very 'First World' dominated. However, it is our hope that Kanamai and the material in this Study can stand alongside Untermarchtal and its material; so that, although this Study does not have a single eucharistic focus, as the Dublin Consultation will have, yet it should provide a marker which the Dublin participants keep carefully in view. I have every hope that the African Provinces will also be represented there in person in some strength, and I am confident that they will find in Kanamai an instrument to assist their own contribution to the marking out of the Anglican liturgical future.

[1] The Untermarchtal papers were published as the Study immediately preceding this present one in this current series—David Holeton (ed.), *Revising the Eucharist: Groundwork for the Anglican Communion: Studies in Preparation for the 1995 Dublin Consultation* (Alcuin/GROW Joint Liturgical Study no. 27, Grove Books Ltd., Bramcote, 1994).

1. Issues of Liturgical Inculturation

by Colin Buchanan

PERSONAL

I count myself very privileged to be asked to attend this Consultation and to give this paper. I have no African qualifications whatsoever, and everybody in this room knows that, and if ever I speak as though I knew anything about Africa you must quickly curb me. There is hardly anyone in the room who knows less first-hand about liturgy in Africa than I do, and it would be absurd for me to be giving you detailed advice about indigenizing your worship in this corner of the continent or that.

So let me tell you what I can bring. I have travelled a lot round the Anglican Communion; I have put together three collections of eucharistic liturgies and one collection of ordination ones from round the Communion; in the process I have corresponded widely; I had a fairly substantial hand in compiling the Church of England's ASB; I was secretary to the Group on Liturgy within the Mission and Ministry section at the Lambeth Conference in 1988; I edit a monthly journal on liturgy (I think it is the only international Anglican one there is)[1]; I have participated in all four International Anglican Liturgical Consultations, and, with my publishing hat on, have published the results of most of them.[2]

1. INTRODUCTION

Let me begin by setting up some questions. I shall not answer all of them, but I suppose that part of the purpose of an opening 'keynote' paper is to identify questions, rather than necessarily to answer them. If I *could* answer them, that would be the end of the week together.

I suppose we shall have to ask ourselves the following questions:

(a) What is culture? The first answer would have to be that it is the whole of life, as seen on a group basis. The group does not have to be geographically tight, nor exhaustive of the people in an area—for instance, it would be true of England's history to say there was a peasant culture and an aristocrats' culture. Either, if brought into the homes and lives of the other, would have felt very alien from the way of life there. But in any one village both could be found.

Now in most parts of the world people are fighting to save or preserve their cultures, even whilst unable to resist the forces which change them. For instance, I was on Saturday with the Maasai who are facing the question: can a village culture be the same as a nomad culture? And yet our identity is bound up with our past and our inheritances—even with the persons of our ancestors. We here have the further task of identifying whether and how

[1] *News of Liturgy*, which has been published monthly by Grove Books since 1975.

[2] See Bishop David Gitari's Introduction on pp.6-7 above.

culture can be preserved in liturgy—and not so much for the culture's sake (which could even be viewed as mere archaizing) as for the liturgy's sake; because, to those whose lives have been revolutionized by Jesus Christ, it is the making of worship living and authentic in the present and in true continuity with our past which has the priority.

(b) How locally distinctive does it have to be to be worth our consideration? (For instance, I live in a multi-cultural parish!) Or, on a larger canvas, is there an African culture, or only a national one, or only a tribal one? And does culture belong with and to language-groups or has it an existence which is independent or semi-independent of the language used?

(c) How far is human culture separable from the religious thought-forms that lie behind it, and sometimes are shot through it, and how far is it inextricably identified with it?

(d) How far should liturgy be culturally specific to a particular area, and how far should it endeavour to be urbanely universal and catholic?

(e) Is the question of inculturation different for second generation Christians from what it is for first generation ones?

2. HAS THE CIRCUMCISION DEBATE ANYTHING TO TEACH US?

I want to look in some detail at the significance of the struggle about circumcision—and the necessity or otherwise of it—in the first fifteen years or so of the church's life. It is fair to say that the nature of the gospel itself was not fully established and grounded until this controversy was over, and many classic writings of the New Testament—particularly Acts, Romans, Galatians, Ephesians, Colossians; and perhaps also Hebrews and 1 Peter—either show the controversy in the process of resolution, or are written in the wake of that resolution.

So let me take you to the Council of Jerusalem in Acts 15. The first Gentiles have been converted a little while back without having to be circumcised and become Jews first, and Peter had faced out the Jerusalem church at the time; and we learn in Acts 11.18: 'When they heard this, they had no further objections and praised God saying "So then, God has granted even the Gentiles repentance unto life."' And the mission to the Gentiles had sprung from that finding, and was implemented from Antioch in the first instance. It is not clear whether, when Barnabas was sent from Jerusalem to Antioch, he came not only to investigate but also to report back—but it is clear that he stopped there, joined the mission, went to Tarsus to dig out Paul, went on the famine visit to Jerusalem with him, and, after returning to Antioch, went off on Paul's 'First Missionary Journey' into what is now Asia Minor, part of Turkey in Asia. It may be that the Jerusalem Church sensed the control of affairs slipping out of their hands, or that they felt out of touch in that they had not had a proper report from Barnabas (who, if this is correct, had forgotten he was supposed to give an account to them), or that they were detecting what they thought to be dangerous tendencies in the Gentile mission. Certainly the Jerusalem church does not seem to have slipped as easily as Paul and Barnabas did into dispensing with Jewish requirements. So we find in Acts 15 first of all (v.1) that some judaizers come down to Antioch from Jerusalem, and Paul and Barnabas are in sharp dispute with them; then (vv.2-3)

Paul and Barnabas themselves travel up to Jerusalem, making themselves allies all the way as they call in on Phoenicia (our Lebanon, I guess) and Samaria (Northern part of our Israel)—they do this simply by recording the conversion of the Gentiles, as far as we are told, but presumably in the process they are preaching a certain freedom to the young churches of new converts, which adds to the gladness of the brothers.

When they reach Jerusalem, they encounter the second round of Jerusalem judaizers. When they report (v.4) 'everything God had done through them', certain Pharisees who were believers attack the way they have been making converts. Their attack takes this form (v.5): 'The Gentiles must be circumcised and required to keep the law of Moses'. It appears likely that this is a two-pronged requirement—circumcision itself would presumably not be called 'the law of Moses', so there are also other matters, matters which we presumably would call ceremonial, where they are not required to obey to the letter. So they hold what we now call a Council. At it Peter refers back to the initial conversion of the Gentiles (his mission), Paul and Barnabas give their own account of the Antioch and Asia mission, James (who is thought to have been chairing the meeting, and was thus giving judgment) then sums up—and sums up decisively in favour of the Peter/Paul/Barnabas gospel, and here are his crucial words: 'We should not make it difficult for the Gentiles who are turning to God.' The letter to the new churches then goes off (vv.23-29), though it is not clear to us exactly what it means—it does not actually mention circumcision, for instance, nor reserve the Ten Commandments as still to be obeyed (though they do crop up later in Paul's letters), but it does have the following comprehensive dispensation 'It seemed good to the Holy Spirit and to us not to burden you with anything beyond the following requirements: You are to abstain from food offered to idols, from blood, from the meat of strangled animals and from sexual immorality.'

If we get back inside what we may fairly infer, the Jerusalem Council was giving judgment to the whole world, whether because they were permanently to give such rulings, or whether because they recognized the need for some immediate authoritative statement, we do not know. But in their handling of it, they made clear that one group in the church were not to inflict matters of taste or prejudice or even unreflective customs on others as necessities.[1]

So the universality of the early church was asserted and preserved by their *not* insisting on customs which might actually be neutral in themselves, but which, if they were made binding upon others, would make the worldwide church somehow Old-Testament-Jewish culture-specific.

Perhaps I can impress this point on the mind by offering you a series of knobbly footnotes to it:

(a) Paul's reference to the issue thereafter does not touch closely upon how the gospel is to be *initially* proclaimed to the Gentiles. He takes *that* for granted.

[1] By the time I came to edit this paper, I had learned much more about circumcision itself, male *and* female, and its continuing importance in some tribal customs in some (though far from all) parts of Africa. I suspect Christians ought to study this actual circumcision controversy of the early church very closely indeed ... (see the Kanamai Statement, Section 3.2, p.43 below.)

No, his problem is that people originally converted through free grace thereafter want to justify themselves by their specific good works, and to bind legalistic requirements upon others. In other words, we have a triple problem with the bias of the human heart: it lapses easily into legalism in itself; it enjoys dictating to others; and it binds its own legalism upon others. And his antidote is always to take them back to the terms upon which they originally became Christians—'having begun in the Spirit, are you made perfect by the flesh?' (Gal. 3.3); and 'Stand fast in the liberty with which Christ has made you free' (Gal. 5.1). I think we need as Anglicans to keep this before our eyes, because we have a particular genius for making a secondary point of preference into a universal rule of conformity.

(b) there is a subtle variant on this principle to be discovered. It looks as though you did not always *have* to stand on your freedom, but could voluntarily make concessions to the other person's scruples or even suspicions—that, I take it, is how we must understand the circumcision of Timothy at the beginning of Acts 16. He voluntarily underwent the operation, but in a purely physical way, not as any form of initiation (he was already a Christian in good standing), *nor* as in any sense becoming a full-blown Jew; but simply as conforming outwardly for the sake of not causing offence to Jews who might be dealing with him. The point that underlies it all is that we may vary or restrict our liberty for the sake of pleasing others, so long as we do not turn that restriction into a legalistic rule about the knowledge of God himself.

(c) We find a kind of halfway house in the second century. Then the controversy is about the date of Easter. The Eastern part of the Mediterranean says it should be on the fourteenth Nisan (i.e. the Jewish passover date—whatever day of the week that happens to be each year—and it will vary like our Christmas) and thus they become Quartodecimans; whilst the Western part of the Mediterranean says it should be on the first day of the week as that commemorates the Lord's resurrection, which is, after all, central to Easter. It looks as though when Polycarp goes to Rome to plead the Quartodeciman case (in 155 or after), the Pope is prepared to recognize him as Christian, to respect his age and saintly courage, and yet agree to differ on this question. However, it looks as though the Westerns are only tolerating the East for the sake of the aged Polycarp, and are quietly determined to bring the East into line as soon as they can, and that does happen over the next forty years. Is the church year which *you* keep a 'cultural' point? Well, not originally—it is at the original point a matter of exegesis or open choice in a new situation, but in the second generation such a custom is part of your culture, even if you cannot show how it is expressive of, or even conformable to, the general run of your psychology or sociology. (You can test that out by asking yourself how you would respond to the idea of having Easter on a different day of the week each year—or the idea of Christmas always observed on a Sunday. Are those traditions our *culture?* I think they are, and the sense of annoyance or even outrage that proposals to change them would cause confirms this.[1])

(d) When Augustine of Rome landed in Kent in 597 AD, he consulted the Pope as to whether he should make the church he was founding conform to Roman norms. Gregory the Great apparently instructed him to respect existing customs, as it was in no way necessary for ceremonies and customs to be everywhere identical, so long as the substance of the faith was held in common. However, soon after that the mission expanding from the South encountered Celtic Christianity spreading from the North-East Southwards into England, and there was a strong sense that the two brands must agree a common way of life. Roman customs prevailed, and Celtic modes were over-ridden. So the Pope's original word to Augustine was clean forgotten.

(e) I shall come to Anglicanism in a minute, but I put down one marker—Article XXX1V of the XXXIX Articles of 1571 says that customs and rites do not have to be identical throughout the world, but that particular and national churches may make their own rules. Curiously, Anglicanism has over the centuries worked this out into practice in respect of provincial constitutions—so that Provinces have total autonomy over their own lives under God, including their liturgical lives—but there is a strong residual run-on from the past in respect of liturgical identity, so that independent Provinces do not think or act independently in respect of liturgy, even though it is not *constitutionally* required that any two Provinces be like each other anywhere in the world. I suspect of course that the 'dependency syndrome' was being morally challenged by Roland Allen at the turn of the century—long, long before there was constitutional autonomy.

(f) There may be a further question as to whether the generations have to be like each other in the same place or in the same country. Whilst what our fathers did may be our cultural expression, paradoxically it *can* be just the opposite—i.e. what they did becomes *their* (quite unconscious) cultural imperialism over us. That also wants thinking through (it has been very important in England in respect of both vernacular language and architecture), and it may bear upon my earlier question as to whether first and second generation converts see with the same eyes as each other.

3. TRADITIONAL ANGLICANISM

So let us begin to look at what happened when Anglicanism expanded with the missionary movement through Africa (though what I say is not unique to Africa). I have four propositions to offer:

Firstly, the 1662 Book of Common Prayer went everywhere with the Bible when Anglican missionaries were at work. Why was that? Well:

(i) Anglican missionaries were themselves usually very loyal to the Book, were themselves convinced that it was better than any other worship book avail-

[1] In passing I can tell you of a motion that once went through the diocesan synod of Christchurch in New Zealand, calling for Christmas Day to be transferred in New Zealand to 25 June, so as to give themselves a mid-Winter holiday. However, the Provincial synod, with a sense of traditions—even of culture—laughed it out.

able in Christendom, had themselves promised always to use the Book, and saw it as being crucial to being Anglican.

(ii) Something you may not have understood well in Africa is that early missionaries were very conscious of the eyes of people in England upon them. So early anglo-catholics started to relish their own liberation from 'uniformity' and to push their own boat out a bit—particularly with advanced ceremonial (not a bit inculturated, but basically following Rome—though sometimes with local art-work, statuary, vestments etc.). Early evangelicals were conscious of fighting court-battles in England over the rubrics of the Book of Common Prayer, so they would not abandon it out here as though they were not serious about it. They saw themselves as bound up with events in England, even when lines of communication were very slow, and conditions under which they were operating very different from England. I once heard A. T. Houghton, the first overseas missionary of BCMS recalling how in 1928 they held a meeting where he was serving to give praise to God at the defeat in the House of Commons of the 1928 Prayer Book—and that prayer meeting was in Upper Burma! I write these lines not to defend evangelical missionaries, but to help you understand them.

(iii) I think it is also a proper question to ask whether the first evangelists from the European missions *could* have provided the first new converts with programmes and materials for truly inculturated worship, even if they had wanted to do so or had dreamt of it. Anyone newly turning to Christ was bound to ask 'Now what do I, what do we, *do*?' No responsible evangelist could ever have replied 'Read your scriptures and write prayers and songs and form an order of service out of your own understanding of your own culture but with Christian content.' Simply to state that alternative programme is to scupper it. A more likely scenario is that a man struggling to learn a local vernacular language (and perhaps to get one Gospel written down and supplied by the Bible Society) would also be saying to the first converts 'Please help me put some prayers—perhaps even some hymns—into your language; then we can worship together.' Or, if it came to a church building, the locals would be saying to the missionary 'What ought a church building to look like?'—and he (or she) would inevitably be giving guidance out of the limitations of his or her own awareness of building designs in England. (That is quite important in the nineteenth century and up till the middle of this century.) If we may be more specific, I cannot see how a convert from animism could be told 'Conserve what is of value to you as an African of this tribe and region, strip it of its animistic connections, and serve it up again but with Christian content.' Or, in a different continent, I do not see how an English missionary in India who agreed with the prohibition of 'suttee' (that is, the burning alive of widows on their husbands' funeral pyres) could then say to an ex-Hindu 'Bring what you can of your previous burial customs into Christian liturgy'. I take it that a true convert would have been learning explicitly or implicitly that his previous culture was totally anti-Christian on the one hand, and was inseparable from its religious force, contents and accoutrements on the other.

(iv) And yet I want to assert that somewhere deep inside Anglicanism is an incarnational principle. We believe that in principle our Christianity ought to be incarnated as of a particular people living in a particular way in a particular place at a particular point in time. Just as Jesus was born as a Jew into a Jewish household and belonged humanly to his own era and people, so the people of God to-day have to belong with the people amongst whom they are set. They must not be so trans-culturated into some other culture that they lose touch with relatives, neighbours and family; and for a new convert to be baptized and belong to a worshipping community should involve the offence of the cross—that is basic to its being the Christian gospel which has been received—but should the convert have to swallow the cost of renouncing the *culture* and taking on a new (and foreign) culture also? Or should it be possible for a new convert to step naturally into truly inculturated worship? So there must be in principle be some limitation or at least some contrary challenge to the mere transfer of the BCP and its attendant culture into a setting of a different people in a different era on a different continent.

Secondly, I want to assert that much English culture and much English church culture was taken for granted by pioneer missionaries. I suspect that their expectation that they would civilize' people (by giving them trousers to wear, individual property to value, tools to use, literacy and Bibles to read) was usually so paternalistic that they simply viewed themselves as casting out the abhorrent in people's lives and filling the empty place with healthful replacements—the Christian gospel plus English cultural accoutrements. There was one glorious exception—one point of true inculturation—one matter in which the sending nation may have some pride: that relates to the use of vernacular language. It was a great point of principle in the English Reformation, and it became a point of principle in the missionary expansion. As a matter of fact the Act of Uniformity of 1662 provided for the translation of the Book into Welsh within a given period of time, an outworking of that principle from the start.[1]

So the overseas usage was all in line with the past history of the Book in England, when overseas not only the Bible but also the BCP were put into the vernacular languages—and, furthermore, as far as I know, there was never an attempt to find the archaic form of a language in order to translate with the same 'stained-glass-window' effect that Cranmer's English prose gave to the English Prayer Book. Much vernacular use of the blessed 1662 in Africa may therefore actually be much more contemporary in its style of language than is the BCP in English in England.

However, the issue of the vernacular stands out marvellously by contrast with nearly everything else. There has been an all-pervasive Anglican sub-culture which has gone everywhere with the missionaries. I instance: robes (and

---

[1] I think it also went into French for the Channel Islands, though it was never then put into Cornish, let alone Irish. *They* had to use English—the language of imperial Westminister.

clericalism), ceremonial, architecture, music (and lyrics), even church-bells, hassocks, brass eagles as lecterns, collecting-bags, murals, candlesticks, choirboys smiling seraphically in ruffs, and a thousand more besides. The particulars of Anglican worship in developing nations are so often the particulars of English Victorian worship. And, if I may illustrate by adding a recollection of my own, I recall a Sierra Leonian student of mine, after he had returned home, sending at intervals to England for wafers to be sent to him by airmail. The bookshop I was running duly supplied them, but we were dismayed at what was happening to Sierra Leone's hard currency. Surely *some* kind of local bread would be available? But the English standards to which my friend was conforming would not have allowed such a thought. I note in passing that the elements used at the eucharist, and the possible variants on them which we may be ready to endorse, are a large cultural question throughout the world.

When I mention the cultural accompaniments of Victorian English church life, I am not only thinking of the visible effects created by what was introduced—such as little wood-gothic church buildings around New Zealand—but also of what was thereby wiped out. It is clear that the cultural change brought by the Christian missions was of a sweeping and uncompromising sort. So it was not only what was brought in that we have to question, but also—and even more—what could have been conserved that was thrown out.

You must yourselves further tell me whether you have in African Provinces the same innate conservatism in church life that we have in England. In other words, it is not only that you have been subjected to enormous cultural imperialism, but that people have come to love things the way they are, and are unwilling to change—and we all have to remember that people who have drawn near to God over many years through a familiar pattern of words and ceremonies may be quite disorientated and reckon they have lost touch with God when the medium is changed. However, we also have to remember that the question is as much one about the cultural expression of Christianity in which our children will be brought up, as it is one about caring for those already in a long-standing rhythm of spirituality.

My third proposition about Anglican worship is that there were usually civil powers, imperial powers, standing behind the missionary endeavours. I cannot tell how far this lent authority to the actions of missionaries (and it would be different in each country—and not every country represented here was colonized from Britain anyway). But I look at Nairobi cathedral and visualize (as is recorded) the foundation-stone of Anglicanism in the capital of Kenya being laid by His Imperial Majesty's personal representative, and reckon the union in England of church and state in some way gave Anglicanism (as known in England) a good push from Caesar in the colonies.[1]

My fourth proposition about Anglican worship relates to the Lambeth Conferences. In 1908 the unity of the Anglican Communion was said to be cemented through the universal use of the Book of Common Prayer (there were one or two

---

[1] I observe at the point of going to press that my friend Solomon Amusan virtually takes for granted the identity of political and liturgical colonialism! See p.51 below.

exceptions to worldwide uniformity even then, but as a general point it was fairly water-tight). The 1948 Lambeth Conference repeated the point. Lambeth 1958 was the first time that serious liturgical revision figures on the Lambeth agenda, and the Conference did acknowledge that liturgies did not have to be identical everywhere, and that independent Provinces were free to revise. However, hindsight suggests that the concerns of that sub-section were driven by the experience of the South India liturgy of 1950 and the awareness of actual revision in progress in Canada, India, Pakistan, Burma and Ceylon, the West Indies, Japan, etc. Most of these revisions were wrestling with delicate problems about exactly the best and right text to be used for the eucharistic prayer, and particularly for the consecration (if that was the right word), the anamnesis etc. There is little sign of a cultural open-ness at all in the revisions under way at that point, and all actual texts up for revision around the world at that time read linguistically like 1662 itself. We could add that when I produced my own three collections of eucharistic texts, covering the years from 1958 to 1985, virtually all I could find with any flavour of indigenization in it was a rubric about *'bell or drum or rattle'* which was in the Papua New Guinea rite in the 1970's (but was omitted in the revision of the early 1980s), and a rubric about the Peace in Korea, which instructed the people to bow to each other (as that is their form of greeting), just as the Maoris in New Zealand may rub noses.[1]

At the 1988 Lambeth two separate resolutions of the Conference as well as six paragraphs within the full statement urge genuine inculturation of the liturgy, and it was those two Lambeth resolutions which were taken as starting points in the York Statement—though the theme of York arose from an earlier determination of the IALC itself, that the issues which Elisha Mbonigaba raised at the 1987 IALC should become the theme of the 1989 one.[2]

4. LITURGY IS NOT TO BE CONFUSED WITH OFFICLAL TEXT

Once upon a time the liturgical text published in the Book was everything, and Anglican worship was exhaustively defined by the words in the Book. But that is not the reality of actual events of worship. In a eucharist only about ten minutes will be official spoken text, and the rest of the time (whether 60 minutes, or 90, or 120) is given entirely to a programme selected and sustained locally—hymns and songs, versions of scripture, sermon (or dance or drama), intercessions prepared locally or even delivered extemporarily, the kiss of Pease (which is quite extensive in some places), and the time taken for communion itself. The character of the rite is further determined by the architecture, furnishings, musical instruments, ceremonial and the sheer numbers and commitment of the people: and none of these are spelled out in the official programme for the rite; they simply happen by local custom or innovation. So you will see I am hesitant

---

[1] See my *Modern Anglican Liturgies 1958-1968* (Oxford, 1968), *Further Anglican Liturgies 1968-1975* (Grove Books, Bramcote, 1975), and *Latest Anglican Liturgies 1976-1984* (SPCK/Alcuin, 1985)—*passim!*

[2] See David Gitari's historical summary on pp.6-7 above.

about simply urging you to have your own provincial Prayer Book—certainly you are free, and may well revise and alter texts, and do so with both independence and creativity, and your worship may become rather more inculturated in the process; but if you recall how much of the rite is *not* controlled by your revision of the ten minutes or so of official text, then you will see how much wider the inculturation question is than what you do with official texts.

5. TRANSCULTURATION

I use a different term because I want it to stretch to two uses. First of all we are looking at the materials of worship. These materials are always all *already* culture-specific in the form they have come down to us (a chasuble is a Roman nobleman's best outdoor dress in the fourth century, I believe . . .), and the lifting of one cultural packaging from it, retaining the abiding gospel content, and repackaging it transculturally, is a delicate operation. All the writers on inculturation I have consulted are clear that a good understanding of the principles upon which the materials you are re-touching or re-drafting are formed is vital to the process of inculturation. 'Doing your own thing' is not an excuse for dropping classic liturgical studies; no, it is a call to understand the history and underlying principles of inherited materials all the more carefully.

Similarly we have to engage critically with the existing local culture. It will be part of the task of this Consultation to open up the rationale of tribal, regional, or national customs (your culture) and see in what ways it is at odds with Christianity, and in what ways it can properly be 'baptized into Christ' and thus provide worship which is incarnational within that tribe or region or nation.

There is another form of transculturation also—that of people. In our world few are sealed in forever to their original village life, but we are modern nomads instead—whether on foot or bicycle, or by bus or aircraft. This fact of itself means that we cannot break the world down into liturgical villages, and we must not encourage too strong a Christian 'village mentality' in our people's minds. They have got to be ready to belong in Christ across cultures, cultures which they value highly, but can also sit light by for the sake of international and cosmopolitan discipleship.

6. SO, ARE THERE ANGLICAN NORMS TO BE FOLLOWED?

Let me begin by sharing with you what I call the Lambeth Conference worship paradox. The day we arrived at Canterbury we were issued with our worship book—it was straight C/E and dull. Then we all received as a free gift a new, music (!) edition of *Hymns Ancient and Modern*, and we were all set up to follow a pattern of worship hardly different from that at Canterbury cathedral down the hill below us. I tried to protest, but was silenced by an English bishop. And so the bishops from the various Provinces plodded through a safe, dull, English routine, almost, it seemed, as though they did not realize they had been hijacked. Some of us were near screaming—we were longing for African songs, Asian ways of praying, Pacific music, etc. Curiously, the Japanese contingent did it best—they got the translators out of their box, formed a choir out of the eight persons they had in all, and led us in something delightfully inculturated.[1]

Even whilst this was going on we were calling, in the section I was in, for true inculturation to happen. I think I ought here to pay tribute to Elisha Mbonigaba's paper which he had read on the subject at Brixen at the second IALC a year before—a paper which had already given a dynamic theme to the Third IALC being planned for York in 1989.[2] Thus we worked on inculturation questions, and the group on liturgy (of which I was secretary) put forward only one motion for plenary adoption, and that was

> 47 LITURGICAL FREEDOM
>
> This Conference resolves that each Province should be free, subject to essential universal Anglican norms of worship, and to a valuing of traditional liturgical materials, to seek that expression of worship which is appropriate to the Christian people in their cultural context.

There were other Lambeth developments—I can only direct you to the report, or to my own booklet, *Lambeth and Liturgy 1988*, and ask you to follow them further.[3] The story I am telling goes on to the Third IACL at York in 1989, where all the papers and discussion were about inculturation, and the statement 'Down to Earth Worship' is in the pamphlet called *'Findings'* whilst the essays are in the green book *Liturgical Inculturation in the Anglican Communion.*[4]

However, I think I ought to pick up words in that Lambeth Resolution and, along with inculturation, encourage you to reflect (as inevitably you must when inculturating) upon what could be 'universal Anglican norms'. I offer a personal attempt at giving a minimal content to that concept:

(a) The principles of a church year, lectionary, and Bible
(b) The principle of liturgical structure and direction
(c) The recognizable preservation of baptism and communion (as biblical)
(d) Congregational intelligibility and participation
(e) Certain set forms—as e.g. the Lord's Prayer.

Finally I ask us whether, if we only had those minimal qualifications in a liturgical life otherwise highly inculturated, would we still be visibly Anglican?

My own answer to my question would be 'yes'. But we also have to ask 'if the answer were in fact "no", would it actually matter?'!

---

[1] The reason for our conservatism proved to be that in 1978 the provinces had all been asked to bring their own materials, so the Americans arrived with a free copy of their fairly expensive new Book of Common Prayer, and gave one to everybody, which was fairly intimidating—so for 1988 the Primates said they wanted to avoid that, and they would like the Archbishop of Canterbury to arrange something—and he appointed a very cautious Scotsman, Alistair Haggart, and he organized a book for worship, only a hands-breadth from very traditional English and Scottish Episcopal uses . . . Let 1998 beware.

[2] I add that his paper which follows mine here greatly reinforces his Brixen salvo.

[3] For Resolution 22 Of the Lambeth Conference, see p.6 above.

[4] As David Gitari records above, the IALCs themselves continued to the Fourth one at Toronto in 1991, and the statement and recommendations from that are in the Grove Booklet, *Christian Initiation in the Anglican Communion*, whilst the essays are in a 250-page book, *Growing in Newness of Life* (ABC, Toronto), and I should add that the Primates and ACC in Cape town encouraged Provinces to study the Toronto document, thus undergirding our work.

2. The Indigenization of Liturgy

by Elisha G. Mbonigaba

INTRODUCTION

The Indigenization of Liturgy is the same topic I presented to the Second International Anglican Liturgical Consultation at Brixen, Italy, in August 1987. Recalling that we were only two representatives from Africa at the Brixen Consultation, I want to acknowledge with appreciation that at the Fourth Consultation which took place in Toronto, Canada, in August 1991, seven delegates represented Africa, four of them being bishops, two clergy and one laity. And today, in attendance we have so many bishops and clergy from all over Africa. I am only sorry I could not be at Toronto myself.

The reason is that at more or less the same time (27 July—6 August 1991) the Episcopal Professors from American Episcopal Seminaries and Anglican Theological Lecturers from Africa met in Harare, Zimbabwe, for a Consultation on the Mission of the Church in Context. I am glad to observe that the organizer and co-ordinator at Harare, the Rev. Leon Spencer is with us here. One of the workshops which I co-chaired with an American Professor (Dr. Ralph McMichael) was 'Liturgy in Context'. Our observation was that Anglican Provinces in Africa were very slow in revising and renewing their liturgies.

In our Harare Communiqué, we said:

> 'The group, however, observed that Anglican Provinces in Africa have been slow in reviewing their liturgies. Most of the Provinces have only translated either 1662 Books of Common Prayer or the alternative service Books in local languages. The Church of the Province of Kenya was cited as one of few exceptions, with revision providing for local expression in its service of Holy Communion. Members therefore emphasized the need for Anglican Churches in Africa to express Context through Hymnody, Prayer and Sacraments like Baptism using traditional names which have meaning vis-a-vis using Western terms. The group noted that Western names, even biblical ones, are not necessarily Christian; rather they come from particular Western and Jewish context.'[1]

I am also glad to note with appreciation, that the Council of Anglican Provinces in Africa (CAPA) which met in Harare in October 1992 endorsed our request to establish a network of Anglican Theological College (institutions) in Africa to nurture and strengthen the Ministry of Theological Education in Context in Africa.

Our meeting here at Kanamai, Mombasa, Kenya, with delegates from most of the Anglican Provinces of Africa, is a sign that a wind of renewal, a wind of change is moving across Africa. I only have to add on the emphasis, and to request ourselves to take inculturation of liturgy seriously.

---

[1] Final report on the Anglican-Episcopal Inter-Seminary Symposium in Africa, Harare, Zimbabwe 27 July—6 August 1991.

HISTORICAL PERSPECTIVE

> 'Africans are notoriously religious and each people had its own religious system with a set of beliefs and practices. Religion permeates into all the departments of life so fully that it is not easy or possible always to isolate it.'[1]

Mbiti's statement is an easy affirmation of faith in African Traditional Religion as being an important and necessary phenomenon of African life—something that has been from the beginning of creation of human beings and the world, as some myths and stories of various tribes indicate. It is not something that has been imported to Africa as some anthropologists and missionaries have said. Mbiti and some other African theologians[2] refuted the early wrong and misguided approach of European and American students of Comparative Religions and African Culture, in particular. These expert anthropologists, missionaries and colonialists, were convinced that Africans did not have anything one could call religion; Africans did not believe in any being you call God, or Supreme Being. Emil Ludwig was quoted saying:

> '... how can untutored Africans know God ... How can this be? ... deity is a philosophical concept which savages are incapable of framing'.[3]

These Western experts[4] dismissed an African as being primitive, native, savage, pagan, animist, totemist, ancestor-worshipper, fetishist, naturalist. He/she was immoral, deceitful, satanic, devilish and criminal. Some Europeans thought that Africans had no soul, no sense of history; therefore Christianity as a historical religion could not easily take root. The problem the experts had was that they approached their study with a Western rational, philosophical, theological mind. True[5] interpretation of symbolic rituals would not be enough without full participation of the researcher and without acquiring the thought-forms of African people. Some of the African symbolic rituals and religious beliefs cannot be rationalized or abstracted by Western rational and philosophical standards.[6] They are dramatized and lived and not verbalized.

Recently there has been a shift from negative study to positive and sympathetic study of African Culture. B. Chango Machyo W'Obanda, a Ugandan politician, puts it in this way;

> 'Contrary to what the present day preachers of the so-called great religions think of Africa, it is this very Africa which is the mother of their religions. It

---

[1] John Mbiti, *African Religions and Philospby* (paperback edition) p.11.

[2] D. B. Danquan, *The Akan Doctrine of God*; E. B. Idown, *Oludumare: God in Yoruba Belief;* J. Mbiti, *African Traditional Religions; Concepts of God in Africa.*

[3] E. Smith (ed); *African Ideas of God*, p.11.

[4] Taylor, *Primitive Culture* (1971); *Religion in Primitive Culture* (Harper Torch Books, 1958); Dunkhem, *The Elementary forms of the Religious Life* (The Free Press, 1915); S. Frend, *Totem and Taboo* (1950).

[5] Victor Turner, *The Ritual Process.*

[6] See, e.g., F. Temple, *Bantu Philosophy*, (English Edition, 1959); E. G. Parinder, *African Traditional Religion* (SPCK, 1954); John Taylor, *The Primal Vision* (SCM, 1963); E. E. Evans Pritchard, *Nuer Religion* (1956); Monic Wilson, *Communal Rituals of Nyakyusa; Religion and Transformation of Society* etc.

is to Africa that they owe not only the idea of God, but even monotheism. The worship of One God . . . the ancient African cultural values and practices which gave birth to present Christianity which has been distorted to serve imperialism.'[1]

African traditional culture is not pagan or primitive or superstitious, as early students of anthropology, missionaries and colonialists used to call it. In fact, it is now being argued convincingly, by both Western and African scholars, that if the Christian church in Africa is to survive and be relevant and effective in her mission to contemporary Africa, she has to adapt to the cultural context.[2] There seems to be a general agreement on the necessity of contextualization if contextualization means making concepts or ideas relevant to a given situation, but what is not agreed upon is the method. The indigenization does not mean to resurrect the negative past, but to acknowledge the positive cultural values and the present realities of social, economic, political and religious factors that influence and condition our life culture is not static but dynamic.

The norms for adapting the Liturgy to the genius and traditions of people by the Roman Catholic Church are contained in Article 37 of the Constitution on the Sacred Liturgy:

> 'even in the Liturgy, the Church has no wish to impose rigid uniformity in matters which do not involve the faith or the good of the whole community. Rather she respects and fosters the spiritual adornments and gifts of the various races and peoples. Anything in their way of life that is not indissolubly bound up with superstition and error she studies with sympathy and, if possible, preserves, intact. Sometimes in fact she admits such things unto the liturgy itself, as long as they harmonize with its true and authentic spirit.'[3]

ANGLICAN RENEWALS

The Lambeth Conferences were very slow to recognize the need for indigenization. They came first to flexibility, as in 1978 the bishops said:

> 'In the past, the Book of Common Prayer was an important unifying factor in Anglican worship . . . We believe . . . unity in structure can rightly co-exist with flexibility in context and variety in cultural expressions for the Holy Spirit is both a spirit of order and an unpredictable wind . . .'

In 1988 Lambeth Conference recognized the need for inculturation of liturgy as shown by the following paragraphs on the liturgical renewal.

---

[1] B. Chango Machyo W'Obabda, *The African Origin of Great World Religions*, (A lecture delivered to the students of the Department of Religious Studies, Faculty of Arts, Makerere University, on 17 February 1993).

[2] E. Mbonigaba, 'Indigenization of Liturgy' in Thomas J. Talley (ed.) *A Kingdom of Priests Liturgical Formation of the People of God* (Alcuin/GROW Joint Liturgical Study no. 5, Grove Books, Bramcote, 1988) p.41.

[3] General ed. Walter, M. Abbott, SJ, Translation ed. Very Rev. Msgr. Joseph Gallagher, *The Documents of Vatican 11*.

[4] *The Report of the Lambeth Conference 1978* (CIO Publishing, London), p.94-95.

Para 181 states:

'yet the liturgy must at the same time give authentic expression to the common life in Christ of the people of God present at each particular gathering, in whatever generation and in whatever country and culture.'

Para 182

'Thus, for instance, the hymnody of each place and time will both express the timeless and universal word of God and express it in a poetic and musical form appropriate to the worshipper ... The Church has to worship incarnationally, ... We affirm expressions of true local creativity within the life of the worshipping community which well up from within the people in response to the stirrings of the Spirit. Thus we recommend and encourage authentic local inculturation of liturgy, and fear lest in many parts of Anglican Communion we have been all too hesitant about it.'

Para 183

'The Anglican Communion cannot of course enforce uniformity, nor, in the last analysis, over-rule an autonomous Province which decides to take a path of brinkmanship (or worse) in its liturgical use. But the Lambeth has some reason to hope that its general principles here will hold, and equally has good reason to treat each Province as responsible.'

Para 185

'The presuppositions of the 1662 BCP itself were of a static "Christendom" England, so that little awareness of mission touches its pages; its requirements of the laity were of largely passive participation, and, for all its ancient beauties, its liturgical structuring has been called heavily into question in Province after Province by scholars, pastors, and worshippers alike ... But once a general direction of change is set, the transition, however painful, is better undertaken then evaded.'[1]

However, it seems there is a fear of change. If at all there is a change, it is very slow. This reluctance of change has earlier been noticed. There is a fear in many countries of losing one's acquired Western 'civilized' identity. David Holeton had observed that, in spite of encouragement from the Anglican Primates meeting in 1983 to the Third World Provinces to engage in liturgical revision, 'the first generation of indigenous leaderships tends to cling closely to the inherited liturgical tradition and with reluctance strays from BCP 1662.'[2] The same observation can be made in some dioceses (particularly in Uganda), who are insisting on reprinting the vernacular Prayer Books of 1662, without any revision. Some Bishops reprimand their clergy when they use white cassock or stoles. For such, the true Anglican vestments are black cassock, black scarf and white surplice.

In the survey that Colin Buchanan made nine years ago, it was only the English-speaking Provinces that had renewed their liturgies and had come up with alternative Service Books.[3] The experimental Liturgies of African Provinces

---

[1] *The Truth Shall Make You Free: The Lambeth Conference, 1988* (ACC, 1989) pp.67-68 and also in Colin Buchanan (ed.) *Lambeth and Liturgy 1988*, pp.10 and 12.

[2] E. Mbonigaba, *Ibid.* quoting from an Unpublished Paper by David Holeton.

[3] *Modern Anglican Liturgies 1958-1968* (Oxford, 1968); *Further Anglican Liturgies 1968-1975* (Grove Books, 1975); *Latest Anglican Liturgies 1976-1984* (Alcuin/SPCK, 1985).

like West Africa, Nigeria, South Africa, Tanzania were either modelled after the 1662 BCP or modern English series 2 and 3 or the 1928 rite, while others including Uganda are still using a translation into local languages of 1662. Buchanan had also observed very few signs of genuinely national cultural patterns in Third World revised liturgies. For example, he states that the rubrics in the New Guinea Liturgy 1970 mentions the use of bells, drums, and rattles, twice in the Eucharistic Prayer. The rubric for the Kiss of Peace, in the Korean Liturgy of 1971 reads:

> *'Each person bows to those next to him.'*

These two instances are the only traces of inculturation he could find.

Since then the Province of the Church of Kenya has come up with an indigenous Eucharistic Liturgy 1989 and Modern Services that include Morning Prayer, Evening Prayer, Baptism, Admission to Holy Communion 1991. In the preface it says:

> 'Now we have a new Liturgy of Holy Communion. This is not a modern translation or even adaptation of the old, nor an importation of liturgical revision from the West, but rather a new liturgy which has grown out of recent developments in African Christian Theology and liturgical research. It is both thoroughly Biblical and authentically African, both faithful to the tradition and refreshingly creative.'[1]

If I may make some observations, like Buchanan, apart from the new text of the prayer at the bottom of page 6; the first version of Gloria on page 14; Litany on page 19; the blessing on page 35; there are only two rubrics which reflect African cultural expression. The first one is on page 14—the rubric says:

> *'This first version of the GLORIA may be accompanied by regular clapping.'*

The second is on page 34 sec 35.

> *'The people accompany their first three responses with a sweep of arms towards the cross behind the Holy Table, and their final responses with a sweep towards heaven.'*[2]

The Third World Provinces, especially those in Africa, need to go beyond those two rubrics. African Christians are tired of what they call stereotype prayers which are fixed. They need more alternative prayers that address their daily needs. The structure should be flexible to allow more singing, with African instruments, dancing and other spontaneous expressions. We do, however, need to congratulate the Province of Kenya; they have something in place.

AREAS OF INDIGENIZATION

Much has been said and written about the significance of African culture. It has become a very important feature in theological and liturgical debates. Necessity of inculturation of Christianity and Liturgy is no longer the issue as the Anglican Consultation in York 1989 endorsed. The issue is how to do it in what areas.

Before we can proceed, there are some questions we need to be clear about. Where is the call for inculturation coming from? Is it from the Lambeth Con-

---

[1] The Church of the Province of Kenya Service, *A Modern Service of Holy Communion* (Uzima Press, Nairobi, 1989).

[2] *Ibid.*

ference? Is it from the missionaries travelling across Africa, like Tovey who said,

'Thus today on travelling to the villages in Uganda (for example), it is possible to find Morning Prayer done in a traditional English African way of worship—a disappointment . . .'[1]

Who is being disappointed? Is it that old man and woman in the rural parish setting? Is it that élite African who had dropped his or her African name in exchange for the English name? Is it the youth who says that the African services are dull and dead (funeral type) hence they leave for other charismatic denominations? Who is really saying that the African Christian liturgy is not authentic? I suspect that Tovey might be right when he says that:

'The objection can be raised that the study of inculturation is another form of imperialism.'[2]

Wherever the voice is coming from, we need to address ourselves to those questions, and others like them: We need to listen, we need to study objectively and sympathetically the cultural, political, economic, social and spiritual context and need of that person, before we can provide him/her with inculturated authentic African liturgy. Liturgy cannot be created by a liturgical committee and imposed upon the congregation. Our product might be rejected as soon as it comes out from the factory.

Having said that, let us briefly survey the areas of inculturation. From the anthropological studies done by people like Van Gennep, Victor Turner, Mary Douglas, *et al.*, we are reminded that African life is marked by key moments like pregnancy, birth, naming, teething, initiation, puberty, marriage, death. It involves sowing, harvesting, hunting, herding animals etc. The associated rituals have been identified as 'rites of passage'. Van Gennep has classified the common characteristics that are found in all such rituals. Inculturation of liturgy will have to include all these various aspects of life, and hence there will be many kinds of liturgies.

AFRICAN LITURGICAL INCULTURATION

Some of us who have inherited the low CMS Anglican traditions devoid of use of symbols and rituals, a legacy of reformation controversy, might find it uncomfortable to adapt some of African expressions in liturgy. Yet it has been well established and acknowledged that African heritage is embedded in the people's rituals and symbolic language with a lot of meaning; and that you cannot understand an African unless you get to terms with his symbolic language.

Uzukwu says that gestural behaviour or language is a pattern of expression older than speech, and each ethnic group has its own unique pattern of gestures which they develop as they interact with the environment.

Uzukwu quotes M Jousse who observed that:

'dance (unity of music and rhythm), poetry (unity of rhythm and recitation), music (unity of rhythm and melody) are forms in which a human community expresses the impact of the universe upon it.'[3]

---

[1] Phillip Tovey, *Inculturation: The Eucharist in Africa* p.5.

[2] Phillip Tovey, *Ibid.*

[3] E. Uzukwu, 'African Symbols and Christian Liturgical Celebration' in *Worship* 65, 2 March 1991.

Africans in their respective ethnic groupings as a social community have that community or body language—the gesture which can only be shared and understood by the same group. It would be wrong, therefore, to impose gestural behaviour from European culture onto Africans.

Indigenization or inculturation of liturgy will have to take into account each community's cultural gestures through which they express themselves. The Christ event since the time of the apostles has been adapted to different cultural, social contexts. We seem to have no choice but to allow Christian gestures to be expressed within each cultural group in order to be meaningful. This will include dancing, rhythm swaying, rhythm tapping, drumming, clapping, ululation, embracing, and other genuine, authentic symbolic gestural language. Uzukwu states that:

> 'African anthropology is not preoccupied with the body as fallen and in need of redemption; rather the body is revealed in gestures.'[1]

Chango Machyo observed that,

> 'today there are many African Christians who consider it sacrilegious to even practise their religion with an African touch. Thus, when Archbishop Muluge of Zambia tried to use African methods of spiritual healing, his fellow African bishops accused him of practising magic. He was imprisoned at the Vatican. But when white priests do the same no action such as that is taken! Instead they are held as Saints.'[2]

Chango Machyo continued to say:

> 'Today the worst enemies of African cultural heritage are therefore African converts to both Christianity and Islam. For them everything African belongs to the world of the devil and is therefore heathen and shameful.'[3]

We do not need to continue being enemies to ourselves. We as Christians, need to take seriously the African traditions, religious beliefs, moral values, social structure, all of which are expressed in symbolic gestural language.

As Uzukwu says,

> 'Liturgical celebration in African symbols offers the Christ to Africans in an appropriate way and offers to the universal church another unique experience and expression of the Christ.'[4]

PRAYER

African traditional religious life was characterized by spontaneous, extempore prayers, poured out from the heart to God; expressing the worshippers' feelings, aspirations, anxieties, worries, pain, suffering and joy. Prayers would be in the form of invocations, supplications, blessings, curses, salutations, greetings and farewells. And, as Mbiti says, these would be uttered at any time and in every place. Mbiti had, categorized the 300 prayers collated from most African tribes into the following groups: Prayers for the day, month and year, for life, health and healing, for man's work; for wealth and prosperity, war and adversity; for

---

[1]. E. E. Uzukwu, *Ibid.* p.100.

[2] Chango Machyo, *Ibid.*

[3] *Ibid.*

[4] E. E. Uzukwu, *Ibid.*

life's journey (i.e. rites of passage), the spirit (remembering the departed); rain; offering, confession and creed; praise, blessing and peace.[1]

All these should be inculturated in African Christian liturgical prayers; because they express African spirituality. Lambeth Conference 1988 recommended flexibility and provision for material written for the occasion. The full text in Para. 186 runs as follows:

> 'Another traditional feature of Anglican rites is their fixedness and even rigidity. We seek now a far greater freedom, which has, its own marks of the Spirit. Whilst a set liturgy properly provides a ground-plan structure and the text of central prayers, yet nowadays it can and should often provide for material written for the occasion, for extemporary contributions, and for singing of items (whether time-honoured hymns or more instant choruses) chosen spontaneously. Provinces should be ready to have basic authorized forms for those central parts of certain rites such as the Eucharist, and for those forms to give a substantial part to the congregation. But they should also provide outline structures into which a choice of materials, already existent or written for the occasion, can be fitted. And we look for further openness still which will encourage the truly spontaneous contributions of spiritually alive congregations.'[2]

The richness of African spirituality that is expressed in such thousands of prayers of all occasions, seasons, and conditions of life should be adapted to African Christian liturgy. Some are in Litany forms and they used to be sung by a leader and the community would 'respond in a song or recitation'. This would encourage participation. These prayers are more authentic and contextual. Some could be adapted as they are and other could be modified. If contextualization means 'making concepts or ideas relevant to a given situation', prayers should be contextualized.

AFRICAN MUSIC

This is the most important area in Africa Christian Church that needs indigenization. All the twenty two dioceses in Uganda use vernacular hymns translated from *Ancient and Modern, Golden Bells*, and other European song books. Most of the western tunes have been retained like, 'Rock of Ages, cleft for me', but others which could not fit with African words like 'Amazing Grace...' could not be translated. Some local compositions are going on, but none have been included in the hymn books for singing in church services, apart from 'Bewayo' which is now included in the Luganda Prayer Book.

The Vatican II recognized the value and the importance of African music, and that of other mission lands, in the Constitution in the Sacred liturgy:

> 'In certain parts of the world, especially mission lands, there are peoples who have their own musical tradition, and these play a great part in their religious and social life. For this reason due importance is to be attached to their music and a suitable place is to be given to it, not only by way of forming their attitudes towards religion, but also when there is question of

[1] J. Mbiti, *The Prayers of African Religion.*

[2] *The Truth Shall Make You Free*, pp.68-69 and Colin Buchanan, (ed.), *Lambeth and Liturgy 1988*.

adapting worship to their native genius. Therefore, when missionaries are being given training in music, every effort should be made to see that they become competent in promoting the traditional music of these peoples, both in schools and sacred services, as far as may be practised.'[1]

From Rome we go to Lambeth. Lambeth 1988 also recognized the need to indigenize liturgical music, in its words: '... a poetic and musical form appropriate to the worshippers ... we affirm expressions of local creativity ...'[2] Paul van Thiel says:

'Practically all African traditional songs have sufficient religious tendency by themselves, and are suitable of being introduced into liturgy without any modification.'[3]

Mbiti writes that singing helps pass on religious knowledge from one group to another and helps to create and strengthen corporateness and solidarity. Dr. Mbuga also says that, for an African, music is

'a natural safety valve, and a kind of dial indicating with great accuracy his thoughts and the incessant fluctuations of his sensitivity, for it is by his music that he can read all his philosophy, all his literature, all his history. In songs he expresses his beliefs, his sense of his duty, his tribal morality, his ambitions etc. In fact, everything that really matters to him. Where else can we touch his religious soul if not in his music?'[4]

Given that the biggest percentage of the rural community still uses oral literature and communication, singing traditional hymns would be an authentic way of teaching and preserving Christian faith, because they are easily committed to memory. As Mbuga says,

'melody and rhythm are the deepest potent agencies of African expression.' Through traditional music, the principle of "Lex Orandi, Lex Credendi" is emphasized'.

The beauty of African rhythm in music cannot be over-emphasized, as Hirmer has recognized:

'In songs, occurs the miracle of rhythmical synchronization between a) text-rhythm, b) melody-rhythm, c) clapping rhythm.'[5]

African music has a lot of melodies that fit every mood, like wedding; mourning, hunting, work, story-telling, fishing, grazing animals, religious ceremonial etc. There are many examples we can cite, but this is enough to illustrate that, if liturgy has to be meaningful to an African, African traditional music has to be adapted. As Mbuga says,

'there never was a language with a ready-made Christian terminology ... It was the Christian message which gave them their new and perfect connection.'[6]

---

[1] Walter M. Abbot, SJ (General Ed.) *The Documents of Vatican II* pp.172-173.

[2] Extracted from the quotation on p.21 above.

[3] Paul Van Thiel, 'Spontaneous Creativity and African Sacred Music' in AFER April 1985 Vol. 27 No. 2.

[4] Dr. Mbuga, *The role of Music in the Catechetical Apostolate in Africa: Dini na Mile* (Revealed Religions and Traditional Customs). Makerere University, Sept. 1965 (unpublished).

[5] G. Riordan and O. Hirmer, 'Liturgical Music', in AFER Jan. 1966 Vol VIII No. 1.

[6] Mbuga, *Ibid.*

So we should not be ashamed to use our traditional music and the traditional musical instruments, and dancing. What is wrong if people danced at the festive days of harvest thanksgiving, wedding, etc? David danced before the ark of God. It was the Christian message which gave them their new and perfect connotation. So, we should not be ashamed to use our African traditional music with traditional musical instruments.

This however, requires African Christian composers who are creative, to compose liturgical melodies.

> 'Only Christians who have acquired an authentic Christian mind will be able to produce this type of Christian art . . . The artist who has no religious faith ought not on any account to put his hands to religious art. His soul lacks the power of seeing what God's majesty demands, what his worship required . . . But the artist whose faith is firm and whose way of life is worthy of a Christian, has the love of God as his motive power and puts to relevant use the artistic ability he receives from the creator. So he will try by every means in his power to express and to put before men the truth he holds and the religion he practises.'[1]
>
> 'To obtain this deal, composers should not have only an authentic Christian spirit but a genuine "liturgical training" should be given to them as well . . . Those who compose music to be performed within the liturgy must have a sufficient knowledge of liturgy itself, from the historical, dogmatic and practical (rubrical) aspects.'[2]

The quotations above challenge us to identify Christian people gifted in African traditional music, and teach them theologically and liturgically to enable them indigenize the authentic African liturgical music.

AFRICAN EUCHARISTIC LITURGY

Much has been written about indigenizing eucharistic liturgy and many experimental services have been drawn up, especially in Roman Catholic churches in Africa. Many African theologians have advocated adapting local food and drinks, instead of bread and wine, for eucharistic elements. I have argued elsewhere[3] in favour of using local food and drinks for reasons of incarnational principle and our economic situation. The historical and geographical particularity of the use of wheat and grape wine has been asserted by many theologians. Uzukwu criticizing the 'Canon' which insists on use of unleavened bread from wheat and wine from grapes says that 'The canon fails to realize that all Christians do not live in the same geographical region . . .' He continues to argue that 'One may express surprise and frustration at the insistence on the use of the produce of a particular geographical area; one may even accuse western church authorities of supporting colonialism and economic imperialism.'[4]

---

[1] P. Van Thiel, 'Tone, Tune in African Sacred Music'. Quoted from *Musical Sacred Discipline* No. 24-25 AFER.

[2] P. Van Thiel *Ibid*, Quoted from Constitution on the Sacred Liturgy No. 121.

[3] Elisha G. Mbonigaba 'Indigenization of Liturgy' *Ibid*.

[4] E. E. Uzuwu *Ibid*.

In 1 Timothy 4, 3-5 we read:

> 'For everything created by God is good and nothing is to be rejected if it is received with thanksgiving, for then it is consecrated by the word of God and prayer.'

Again Uzukwu says that the food and drink which is the work of African human hands and which nourishes human kind should be the symbols which should not be denied the function of communicating the mystery of the Christ-event. He states:

> 'all that the Africans eat and drink, the labour of their hands produced in the land bestowed on them by God, are brought to the sacred meal (Eucharist) where the community becomes one with Christ through eating the bread made from the produce of the land (as the body of Christ) and drinking the wine from the region (as the blood of Christ).'[1]

During the time of Amin in Uganda, when imported wine could not be got because of lack of foreign exchange, the House of Bishops of the Church of Uganda allowed the use of banana juice in some dioceses. And Christians had no problem with it. The debate about inculturation of the elements of bread and wine continues; for there is a good number of African theologians who are in favour of indigenous food and drink; those against want to maintain the words of Institution in the Scripture: '. . . this is my body and this is my blood . . .' For them, the word 'this' means not only the gestures of breaking and eating bread and drinking wine, but also the specific element used in that action.

In the Lord's Prayer, 'Give us today our daily bread' refers to daily food that sustains the body, but not necessarily to bread from wheat flour. In Africa, apart from economic considerations, we need to note seriously the theological significance of the whole eucharistic action in the context of a community meal, which conveys meaning to African situations. The rite of eating and drinking together in Africa is a rite of incorporation, it is a sacrament of communion.

OTHER RITES AND OCCASIONAL SERVICES

The contents, structure and prayers of 1662 BCP are too rigid. They were not meant for African worshippers. Pastoral offices are limited and are inadequate to meet the cultic and spiritual needs of African worshippers. As has been pointed out, there are many moments in the human life of an African which are celebrated, like: birth, naming[2], weaning, initiation, betrothal, marriage, entering a new house, death, post-burial ceremonies. With regard to marriage African cultural dress should be used instead of our importing suits and white gowns from England. Local food like millet bread, matoke, etc should be used instead of five-step wedding cakes! At my brother's wedding in July 1991, I insisted on using millet bread. It was put in traditional baskets, cut with a special grass blade. People appreciated the change.

---

[1] E. E. Uzukwu, *Ibid.*

[2] Chango Machyo says: 'the symbol of rejection of everything African starts with dropping of African names and adopting foreign ones in the name of religion.'

Naming is related to liturgy in rites of passage, and we need *African* names as Christians. In my paper at Kanamai I opened this up more.

Besides being traditional, using African costumes and food is less expensive for the newly married couple. For all these new liturgies, they should adapt the richness of the ceremonial rituals that are characterized by the rites of separation, rites of transition and rites of incorporation.

Other areas that would need indigenization are: liturgical space, furnishings, vestments and art. The present architectural setting is based on a Roman basilica or cross-type, a long nave, chancel, and sanctuary; this three-fold division of the Church gives the impression that those in the sanctuary are nearer to God. Those at the back in the nave remain passive as spectators. The lockable building gives the impression that worship and God are confined and locked in the building for the six days and let free on Sundays. African liturgical space should be designed according to the sensitivity and gestural needs of the people. Fixed pews would not allow free, spontaneous worship.

Some suggestions of inculturating Holy Week liturgy have been given by Joseph G. Mealey, from a Roman Catholic point of view. He mentions a priest riding a donkey on Palm Sunday; washing of feet on Maundy Thursday, dramatic reading or play on Good Friday; Outdoor procession with local stations marked at different places in the village, Easter play.

Acting the mysteries of Christ in an African way, in music, drama and dance would encourage participation and would make it relevant to the congregation. Any form of adaptation to make worship contextual should be encouraged.

PROBLEMS OF INDIGENIZATION

Africa and our individual states, dioceses or Provinces are multicultural and multi-lingual except Rwanda and Burundi. Each Ethnic group has its own pattern of gestural communication, symbols and languages. According to Uzukwu, gestural languages must refer to a specific community to be meaningful and one has to return to the ethnic group to recognize oneself and to act meaningfully. In view of this it would not be easy to make one Provincial authentic African liturgy. One has to come up with different liturgies to cater for different unique gestural expression and symbols. The problem of language is two-fold. The Africa liturgist has to use English, a foreign language, translating from African concepts languages and symbols; and then translate back into various ethnic languages. In the process of translating from African language to English, and back to local languages, authentic meaning will be lost. There is a danger of imposing one's ethnical culture over another.

CONCLUSION

Indigenization cannot be achieved unless there is training. Joseph V. McCabe has said that responsible cultural adaptation of liturgy requires adequate personal training in the liturgy, theology and tradition of the liturgy. Article 14 of the Constitution on the Sacred Liturgy sums it up clearly:

> 'In the restoration and promotion of sacred liturgy, this full and active participation by all the people is the aim to be considered before all else; for it is primary and indispensable source from which the faithful are to derive the true Christian spirit. Therefore, through the needed programme of

instruction, the pastors of souls must zealously strive to achieve it in all their pastoral work. Yet it would be futile to entertain any hopes of realising this goal unless the pastors themselves, to begin with, become thoroughly penetrated with the spirit and power of the liturgy and become masters of it. It is vitally necessary, therefore, that attention be directed, above all to the liturgical instruction of the clergy.'

With regards to music, Roman Catholic Church Article 115 emphasizes the importance of practising music in seminaries, in the novites and houses of study of religious, and also in the Catholic Institutions, Schools. To impart this Instructions, teachers are to be carefully trained. It is desirable also to found higher institutes of sacred music wherever this can be done. Composers and singers, especially boys must also be given a genuine liturgical training . . . therefore, when missionaries are being given training in music, every effort should be made to see that they become competent in promoting the traditional music of these people both in schools and sacred services, as far as may be practised.

For our brothers and sisters of Roman Catholic tradition, liturgy and music are mandatory and are to be taught by competent people in theological colleges, schools and parishes. We Anglicans in Africa need to learn from them, and take liturgy and music seriously if the inculturation process is to progress. How many qualified committed Christian musicians do you have in your diocese, or province? How many qualified liturgists? Do we have any Anglican Institutions in Africa where liturgy and sacred music can be specialized in? Our sharing and our need for mutual help should seek ways and means of promoting training in this field. It would be a shame if we continue inviting overseas experts to come and help us in designing African liturgy.

At this juncture our overseas consultants and observers should encourage their home churches to provide scholarships to enable African Churches to specialize in the field of liturgy.

3. The Kanamai Statement

AFRICAN CULTURE
and
ANGLICAN LITURGY:

The Report of the Kanamai Consultation on this theme (31 May to 4 June 1993), with an Introduction by Bishop David Gitari

(The Consultation was convened by Bishop Gitari under the aegis of the Council of Anglican Provinces in Africa (CAPA).)

1. INTRODUCTION

I am glad to introduce the report of the first CAPA Consultation on Liturgy which has successfully completed its work. The Consultation was held at Kanamai near Mombasa, Kenya from 31 May to 4 June 1993. Seventeen delegates from ten of the twelve African Provinces participated in the Consultation.[1] The Provinces represented included Burundi, Central Africa, Kenya, Rwanda, Southern Africa, Sudan, Tanzania, West Africa, Uganda and Zaire. Two Provinces were not represented at the Consultation, Nigeria and Indian Ocean. The Consultation was privileged to have six consultants who are distinguished liturgists. These included the Rev. Paul Gibson of the Anglican Church in Canada, the A.C.C. Co-ordinator for Liturgy, Bishop Colin Buchanan, the Revs. Roger Bowen and Martin Dudley from England; the Rev. Robert Paterson from Wales, and Dr. Janet Hodgson of U.S.P.G. from South Africa. Twenty members of the Liturgical Committee of the Church of the Province of Kenya were also present in their capacity as the hosting committee. Hence the Consultation was attended by 43 participants.

[1] The delegates were:

Burundi	Rev. Anastace Kajugiro Bishop Pie Ntukamalina	**Sudan**	Rev. Gordon Tikiba
Central Africa	Rev. Canon Elson Jakazi	**Tanzania**	Bishop Mdimi Mhogolo Rev. John Simalenga
Kenya	Bishop David M. Gitari Ven. Samson Mwaluda	**Uganda**	Bishop Yoram K. Bamunoha Rev. Elisha Mbonigaba
Rwanda	Bishop Norman Kayumba Bishop Jonathan Ruhumaliza	**West Africa**	Bishop Robert Okine
Southern Africa	Ven. Themba Vundla Rev. Cynthia Botha	**Zaire**	Canon Munege Kabalore Rev. Ian Tarrant

I was privileged to be entrusted by CAPA with the task of convening this Consultation. At one time the Consultation was nearly postponed indefinitely owing to lack of funds to pay air tickets for delegates. However, the CAPA Conference held in Harare in October last year gave encouragement for the planning of the Consultation to go ahead and urged the Provinces to support the Consultation by paying the air fare for their respective delegates. The delegates from African Provinces who attended the ACC and Primates Conference in Cape Town in January this year also gave similar encouragement. On behalf of all the delegates, I wish to thank the ten Provinces which were represented at Kanamai for facilitating their representatives to attend the Consultation. We are also grateful for a grant of Sterling £3,000 from USPG and a grant of Sterling £2,000 from CMS, England. These generous grants enabled us to pay for accommodation and meals of the participants and for other expenses.

2. LITURGICAL RENEWAL IN AFRICAN PROVINCES

We understand that this was not only a unique event as far as Africa is concerned, but that in other parts of the world also there have been few if any regional Consultations of Anglican liturgists of a comparable sort. It has been a joy to us to break new ground. The theme of the Consultation was 'African Culture and Anglican Liturgy'. After two opening lectures on 'Liturgical Inculturation' (one by Bishop Colin Buchanan and one by the Rev. Elisha Mbonigaba of Uganda), the Consultation received reports of Liturgical Renewal from the Provinces. We were encouraged to learn that in nearly every Province some progress was being made in Liturgical Renewal. However, only the Church of the Province of Southern Africa has a new Prayer Book published in 1989. The Church of the Province of Kenya has two liturgical booklets; The Kenya Service of Holy Communion publsihed in 1989 and Modern Services published in 1991 which includes Morning and Evening Prayer, Baptism, Admission to Holy Communion, Confirmation and Commissioning. The new Service of Holy Communion has been drafted for the Church of the Province of Uganda but has not as yet been approved. The Church of the Province of Tanzania adopted a new order of Holy Communion some years ago. The Church of the Province of West Africa is currently working on a new eucharistic liturgy. Even if not much has been published, there is already much liturgical inculturation in various parishes and dioceses throughout Africa. Most of the Provinces, however, still use translations of the 1662 English Prayer Book.

3. WORKING GROUPS ON CULTURE AND LITURGY

The Consultation was divided into five working groups to address five areas where inculturation is an apparent urgent need and opportunity. The five groups took areas as follows:

1. Principles and Guidelines
2. Eucharist
3. Birth and Initiation rites
4. Betrothal and Marriage rites
5. Death and Burial rites

The reports of the five groups were scrutinized and amended by the whole Consultation and were then adopted by members unanimously. Whilst we encountered together a vast variety of African cultures, there was also unity of mind and purpose in the Consultation to enable worship to be truly African, indigenous to every place and people among whom it is celebrated. This would fulfil the terms of the Lambeth Conference Resolution 47 of 1988:

> 'This Conference resolves that each Province should be free, subject to essential universal Anglican norms of worship, and to a valuing of traditional liturgical materials, to seek that expression of worship which is appropriate to the Christian people in their cultural context.'

This was in turn reinforced by the recommendations contained within the statement 'Down to Earth Worship' which was agreed by the Third International Anglican Liturgical Consultation held at York in England in 1989.

4. SOME RECOMMENDATIONS BY THE CONSULTATION

During the final plenary session on Friday 4 June 1993, the following recommendations were made:

4.1 That a CAPA Liturgical Consultation be held every three years. That the next Consultation be held in or about May or June 1996.

4.2 That before the next Consultation, the Provinces be encouraged to work and, if possible, publish the following liturgies (if they do not have them already):
(a) Daily and Sunday Worship (i.e. Morning and Evening Prayer).
(b) Holy Communion.
(c) Christian Initiation (i.e. Baptism and Confirmation).
(d) Church Weddings and Blessing of Customary Marriages.
(e) Burial Service.

4.3 That the second CAPA Consultation shall concentrate more on giving guidelines on the liturgies for:
(a) Making of Deacons
(b) Ordination of Priests
(c) Consecration of Bishops and
(d) Other Occasional Services

4.4 That all the Provinces be urged to support the funding of CAPA Liturgical Consultations and especially the payment of air tickets for the delegates.

4.5 *CAPA LITURGICAL COMMITTEE* The Consultation appointed five delegates present to form the CAPA Liturgical Committee which was given a mandate to plan for the next Consultation:

Region	Name	Office
East Africa	Rt. Revd. Dr. David M. Gitari	Convenor/Chairman
Southern Africa	Ven. Themba Vundla	Vice-Chairman
Central Africa	Canon Elson Jakazi	Secretary
Francophone	Rt. Revd. Jonathan Ruhumuliza	Treasurer
West Africa	Rt. Revd. Robert Okine	Member

Deaconess Joyce Karuri, the Director of Communications in the Diocese of Kirinyaga, Kenya, was appointed Minutes Secretary.

5. LIMITATIONS AND OPPORTUNITIES

There were many limitations upon our Consultation. Not all the Provinces were equally represented; time was inevitably short; and subjects could not be investigated in much depth. We know that there is a vast Christian experience in other Churches in Africa—both historic denominations and African Independent or indigenous Churches—experience which has often taken inculturation far more seriously and for a much longer period than we have. We need to learn humbly from them. We noted in particular that the Roman Catholic Church is further ahead in liturgical inculturation than the Anglican Churches in Africa. Despite these limitations, Kanamai gave many wonderful opportunities. As we gathered on the shores of the Indian Ocean, we enjoyed the cool breeze from the Ocean. The heavy downpour and the stormy waters of Indian Ocean reminded us of some politically stormy parts of Africa. While at Kanamai we heard the news of the election of a new President of Burundi. The sheer fact of being together to share what our different African cultures have to teach us and how we can enrich our worship from what we have inherited from the past was a wonderful and memorable experience.

6. CONCLUSION

We look forward with good hope, for we are learning from each other, and sharing a unity of purpose in Christ Jesus. We hope that under the auspices of CAPA further such initiatives can be taken; and we depend upon Almighty God to bring that to pass. It is our hope that Primates and indeed all the Bishops of the Anglican dioceses in Africa will give the CAPA Liturgical Committee the support and encouragement it needs. Even more important is the hope we have that this first CAPA Liturgical Consultation will encourage Liturgical Renewal throughout Africa and that our work may also have something to contribute to the whole Anglican Communion.

I wish to thank all the participants for the enthusiastic and joyful entering into the task. We also owe a debt of thanks to USPG and CMS in London who provided grants without which the Consultation could not have been held. We are grateful to the members of the Local Planning Committee from the diocese of Mombasa who worked tirelessly to make the conference a success. We thank God for his presence with us and give our work into his hands. We were reminded of the Swahili saying 'HAIWI, HAIWI, HUWA' ('it does not happen, it does not happen, it happens!'). To God be the glory for what has happened.

Rt. Revd David M. Gitari, Convenor/Chairman
First CAPA Liturgical Consultation
On behalf of the Participants

THE KANAMAI STATEMENT

incorporating

REPORTS FROM THE GROUPS

1 PRINCIPLES AND GUIDELINES FOR LITURGICAL RENEWAL

1.1 OBSERVATIONS

Inculturation has always played an important part in the formation and transmission of the gospel. We affirm the Lambeth 1988 resolutions on 'Christ and Culture' and 'Liturgical Freedom', and the 1989 York statement, 'Down to Earth Worship'.

In the light of this, we note the following issues for consideration:

i Those developing new liturgies should:
  (a) *Listen* to the needs of, and consult with, the whole body of worshippers, young and old, male and female, rich and poor, rural and urban, the literate and the non-literate: what do they want to express before God, and how?
  (b) *Exercise caution* in view of the diversity and dynamic nature of African cultures: what helps one group today, may hinder another, or may be out of date tomorrow.
  (c) *Seek insights* from the work done by other Churches in the area, bearing in mind the liturgical convergence seen in the last few decades.
  (d) *Understanding* the principles employed by the Christian liturgists of the past, and the principles of worship in African traditional religion.
  (c) *Recognize and study* the liturgical inculturation which has already taken place, formally and informally, in the previous generations, as liturgies have been created, transmitted and used.

ii There is a need for teaching and training so that:
  (a) *Every Christian* may fully understand the words and symbols used, and so be inspired to worship God in all he or she does.
  (b) *Leaders of Worship* may be sensitive to those whom they serve, and to the symbols and values of local cultures, and may best utilize the tools they are given.
  (c) *Liturgical Specialists* may appreciate the structure of our liturgical inheritance, knowing what may be built up, and what may be safely demolished.

iii Amongst Clergy and Laity alike there are many who fear change or fear losing their identity as Anglicans, or as members of a particular group within Anglicanism. May we all be open to the leading of God's Spirit, and seek our security in the one whom we worship, rather than in the forms of worship themselves.

1.2 MODELS FOR INCULTURATION

Procedure:

Rather than start with the text, it is best to identify the structure of an inherited liturgical tradition, within which one can build creative innovation ensuring inculturation. In contrast to the Roman Catholic Church, we have no central liturgical text which we can adapt.

Nevertheless, a structure for the Eucharist could be as follows:

1 gathering together
2 telling the Christian story with intercessory prayer
3 the meal with thanksgiving
4 sending out

Each part will have its own sub-culture. It is important for people to discover the structure of the Eucharistic Prayer, and compose their own within that framework, rather than translate from English language sources.

Examples

1. The Christians in the New Testament described themselves not as *thiasos* or one of the many words used for religious groups, but as *ekklesia,* a word in common use, both in the Septuagint to describe the congregation of Israel, and also in the secular world to describe the assembly of citizens called by authority to meet in a central place (see Acts 19.30). The Christians were therefore employing the language of the local secular culture to show that they were the people whom God has called into the market place of the world, to declare the Lordship of Jesus Christ.
2. In Latin America in the 1960s, many priests and nuns discovered 'a new way of being with the people', by meeting with grass-roots groups of poor peasants in rural areas and the dwellers in the shanty towns of the cities. They listened in solidarity with them (instead of just coming to teach). In this way they discovered ways of taking joint action (*praxis*) to redress the injustices of society. As they worked for justice, they found themselves also discovering a new theology from the bottom up. It is called Liberation Theology.

   This did not primarily affect liturgy (though it did affect the way the Eucharist was celebrated)—but it can serve as a model for liturgical inculturation. By being with the people in solidarity, the leaders and experts can listen, and so discover new forms and symbols authentic to the grass-roots culture. By this means inculturated liturgy will emerge.
3. In South Africa, there is a wide variety of material, including liturgical forms, in the Ntisikana tradition. Ntisikana (1790-1821) composed the Great Hymn using the literary form of a praise poem, traditional Xhosa wedding music, and a wealth of African symbols to praise God in a Christian context of worship. The point of departure is the African tradition, and it is in dialogue with the incoming culture and Christianity, Xhosa myth story, legend, wisdom, music, dance etc., become 'carriers of change' as they take on new meaning in the Christian context. As a living tradition it has continued to respond to the needs of African people over 190 years.

1.3 GUIDELINES FOR PREPARING NEW LITURGIES

Preparations (not necessarily in this order):

—Identify people who have received or who should receive specialist training.
—Identify the communities which will use the liturgy.
—Listen to the people.
—Choose a working group.
—Set clear and achievable objectives.

Steps for implementation:

1 Agree on principles and structure for the liturgy
2 Write draft texts including:
   —spoken words, actions, music and symbols
   —optional material:
   —scope for local creativity
3 Experimental use together with education
4 Listening to reactions
5 Revision of the texts
6 Adoption by a representative body
7 Training of worship leaders
8 Periodic revision in the light of feedback

Issues Arising

(a) The fact that each liturgy is part of a bigger whole must be kept in mind. Though inculturation of various articles may differ from culture the liturgical structure must be seen not to differ too much.
(b) African liturgists were challenged to do research on different styles of worship in the African culture in order to come up with well blended African Christian liturgies.
(c) For purposes of universality (and possibly uniformity) we ought to understand the principles applied by Christian liturgists of the past and principles of worship in African culture.

2. EUCHARIST AND CULTURE

2.1 INTRODUCTION

We take 'culture' to mean 'cultural trends' since Africa does not have a unified culture. Changes in eucharistic liturgies need now to be thorough, not cosmetic. A serious challenge must be faced. The process recognized as Indigenization—Adaptation—Inculturation (Atta-Baffoe and Tovey) has reached the second phase in Africa, generally, and, where this is so, it is ready to move to the third. Up to this point, liturgical renewal has been more a matter of adapting previously given forms. Moving on to the third phase is a lengthy process.

In drawing up eucharistic liturgies, each province should carefully examine the relevant cultural practices of its nation or region as they might affect eucharistic worship or reflect upon it. In the process of drafting eucharistic rites, provinces should judge whether the cultural practices it has defined can be affirmed in the liturgy.

In drafting, provinces need to allow for local variations within their area of responsibility by providing for flexibility. Provinces should recognize that suggestions made in this report are not recommendations for implementation but are intended to raise questions and issues of importance.

2.2 THE SPIRIT OF AFRICAN WORSHIP

Africans do not only spectate; they participate. The liturgy needs to be open to opportunities for the expression of joy and suffering, of death and hope, affirming people's deepest affections.

One of the problems we face is the mentality which exisiting buildings have created, changing attitudes and restricting buildings have created, changing attitudes and restricting freedom of expression. Architectural features, such as pulpits, can be a problem in certain contexts. Some thought needs to be given to the shape and atmosphere of our buildings, providing spaces for the expression of the Church as the body of Christ, and at no time is this more important than at the eucharist. Alongside this needs to be an appreciation of the nature of holiness associated with places and buildings, and an awareness of the negative fears that need to be combatted. There is a real need for African art, sculpture, woodcarving etc. in our churches. It would appear that the wealth of artistic talent (as well as the artistic offerings of children) could be used to a greater extent.

2.3 MUSIC

We encourage the use of local words and music to make worship more joyful and authentically African. Attention needs to be given to creative writing and composition. Music should not appear to decorate the liturgy but should be regarded as being integral.

2.4 ATTIRE

There is a longstanding tradition that liturgical leaders, particularly those who preside, should wear distinctive clothing which symbolizes their role on behalf of the community and the community's identity in and with them. While such vestments should follow a similar, and therefore recognizable, pattern in a given area, in both style and material they may be drawn from local patterns of ceremonial dress.

2.5 DETAIL

For the purposes of this paper, the eucharist may be divided into seven elements. Before proceeding to outline these elements, it needs to be stressed that provinces should discern the shape of the liturgy before proceeding to detail.

1. The greeting

Lively worship may be encouraged before (and after) the liturgy itself. It is a common practice in many African cultures to greet the gathering before the business begins. The eucharist might begin with greetings as a way of encouraging one-ness at the outset. These greetings should be real, rather than a formality.

The call for Peace (and the greeting of peace) is very important and the best place for it in each rite needs to be found. Wherever it is placed (even if in place of a greeting) it is important to recognize that the 'peace' is much more than a greeting.

2. Penitence

There are a number of possible positions for this penitential element in a eucharistic liturgy. At present it would appear that we use too many words in confession of sin. We recommend the use of silence, singing, gestures, appropriate symbolic acts and any other means to lead worshippers away from sin into a deeper relationship with the Lord. There are African ways of expressing penitence and the church in each setting needs to explore them.

3. Proclamation of the word

The divine authority of the word needs to be stressed with the use of local customs. For instance, in some cultural groups, when a person gives an important message in a gathering, that person uses a staff which symbolizes authority in the community. This kind of custom might be brought into the proclamation of the word, and each area needs to discern its own local practice.

Sometimes the provision of lectionary readings themselves may be too long for the people to concentrate on them. The readings might be shortened, dramatized, danced, memorized, drummed etc.

4. Intercession

When we have heard and responded to the word, we bring the world before God. Nothing is beyond the scope of prayer. Posture and gestures in prayer vary from one cultural tradition to another and the natural form needs to be discerned. Liturgical provision may need to reflect this diversity. How do Africans—or the people of a certain area—normally express themselves in prayer? Some close their eyes and bow their heads, some look at something, some stand, others sit, some kneel, some raise their hands. Again we note that our texts for intercession are sometimes too wordy. We should consider a wider range of styles, including chanting, music and led extempore prayer. This will involve further education of worship-leaders and people.

5. Eucharist

No attempt should be made to follow a set pattern, though provinces should be familiar with the basic elements of eucharistic prayer in the wider church. It may be right to lay more stress on the doctrine of creation and to express the close affinity which Africans feel for the whole created order.

We wish to encourage local people to produce the eucharistic bread and ask the provinces to consider whether they should permit the use of local staple foods and drinks for the eucharistic elements, also carefully considering this alongside the biblical tradition.

6. Sacramental eating and drinking

As much as we respect our cultures, it is necessary to stress the importance of the unity of the family of God and, therefore, to encourage men and women to come together to the Lord's Table. Occasionally, a common-meal might be celebrated and provision for this (guided by biblical principles) might be made if provinces so decide. It would not be inappropriate for the consecrated bread and wine to be passed around the people on some occasions, rather than being served by the ministers.

*7. **Dismissal***

It would seem to be vital that the two elements of continuing in the Church's fellowship and sharing in God's mission should both be expressed in the dismissal.

2.6 CONCLUSION

In all of the above, it will be necessary to combine new thinking and practice with a clear and careful process of education throughout each province.

Issues Arising

(a) Consider the practice of communion meal whereby the Holy Communion or the Lord's Supper is administered in the context of a meal—presumably that is the way our Lord Jesus did it. The supper began like a meal and it was only later that Jesus took up the cup and blessed it.

(b) The greeting factor—greetings should come at the beginning and must be as natural a gesture as possible.

(c) The minister does not necessarily have to use a pulpit, especially in nomadic environments where a 'dialogue sermon' might appeal more to the Christians than a pulpit sermon.

(c) Probably the time has come when local foods and drinks could be substituted for wafers and wine.

(d) Architectural structure of churches needs looking into, as well as artwork.

3. BIRTH AND INITIATION RITES

3.1 BIRTH RITES

The group began with comparing the birth rites of the different areas represented. The traditional birth rites had very much in common including very often a period of seclusion of the mother and child, the coming out ceremony, the naming of the child by either the women, men or special members within the family. There is also a form of ceremonial welcome into the life of the family. There were other practices that are mentioned in T. J. Vundla's paper which had been given to the members of the conference.

The group considered the various practices from a Christian standpoint and concluded as follows:

(a) The practices that were described could easily be brought within a Christian context. They created no problems of heresy or syncretism.

(b) We consider that in many ways Christian liturgy could be incorporated into these ceremonies and enrich them rather than diminish them.

(c) In some Provinces there already exist a thanksgiving service after child-birth which is generally used in Church. The use of this could be extended, and liturgical provision be made for a pastor visiting or a family gathering for prayer at a point appropriate to the birth rites.

(d) We concluded that the whole of the birth-rites considered above fell under the sphere of creation and natural order and they should not be confused with baptism which fell within sacramental and spiritual order. In view of this baptism should take place after the preparation of parents and godparents.

(e) We were made aware of many Christians with infant baptismal problems. The issues concern both the age of Baptism and method used (that is, pouring rather than dipping). We ourselves believe in baptizing infants of believing parents, and we also affirm the rightness of simply pouring water. We note that the Prayer Book allows dipping and pouring.

3.2 PUBERTY RITES

Traditional puberty rites were shared among the members of the group. The rites vary from one group to another and also they are done on both men and women. For men it was noted that rites like cirumcision, tribal marks were prevalent. The reasons for these practices are also varied. The practices in principle are neutral but the rites that accompany the practices need careful examination before they are accepted as an ideal way to prepare men for responsible adulthood.

For women a number of puberty rites also exist. Among the many, clitoridectomy was cited. It was said that the practice had moral social values. The practice varied from one place to another. The risks involved were shared especially at the time it is done, but far more important is the damage it inflicts on a woman's body for the rest of her life. The reasons for such a practice need reviewing so that a proper teaching is given to the Christians with a view to end the practice.

3.3 CONFIRMATION

The rite of confirmation was also discussed. We were of the opinion that the puberty rites should not necessarily be linked up to confirmation. The reason for this is made evident when confirmation is not only done at puberty but when there are also people who are confirmed as adults. Secondly we faced the issue of admitting infants to communion before confirmation (Toronto Statement), a practice which is already going on in one Province and is being experimented with in another Province. This involves quite a change from the received Anglican tradition. The change needs careful study and research by the Provinces before it is done.

This acceptance of those who have been baptized to communion should not hinder confirmation instructions and also confirmation itself.

3.4 BAPTISMAL LITURGY

We were not able to come up with the outline of a baptismal liturgy but we have the following recommendations to make:

1 Each province conduct research on the birth rites and do a Christian evaluation of them to affirm them, if possible make a liturgical provision for them.

2 Each province conduct researches on puberty rites and the rationale behind them with the view to improve, implement and teach Christian morals.

3 Adequate preparations for parents and godparents be done before baptism.
4 We favour the Toronto recommendations on admission of infants to communion after teaching the congregation.
5 We affirm that baptism is a full sacrament of initiation; confirmation is secondary.
6. We recommend that, quite apart from confirmation, pastorally sensitive ways of renewing baptismal vows in or near adulthood be adopted for the sake of various needs including those who desire 'rebaptism'.
7 Each province is free to decide teaching material for confirmation but material should prepare the young people for responsible adulthood.

Issues Arising

(a) Each province needs to do research on birth rites and puberty rites and rationales behind them and their implication on inculturation and liturgical renewal.
(b) Provinces need to study female circumcision more carefully, and tolerantly educate those involved on the ills of the practice.
(c) The group wholly reaffirmed the Toronto declaration on admission to Holy Communion, that baptism is enough, and confirmation is secondary.
(d) Role of bishops needs re-affirming. It is not just confirmation and the bishop should not feel threatened if confirmation was scrapped (though this is not intended). Yet one may wonder why a derived rite (i.e. confirmation) should be made an episcopal rite by the church.

4. BETROTHAL AND MARRIAGE

PREAMBLE

The group assigned to discuss betrothal and marriage in African cultures was also requested to recommend how new liturgies on marriage could incorporate various aspects of African culture. It was noted there was much in common in various African cultures though there were differences in the way marriage was celebrated. In all cultures it was noted there was a stage of betrothal which was reached after essential cultural preliminaries such as request of consent of parents and negotiation of dowry, and the actual betrothal was marked by a climax celebrated culturally. The period of betrothal varied and the actual marriage took place in various ways in different cultures. From what we have learnt from one another, we wish to recommend for liturgical purposes the following points:

1 Recognizing that marriage is a family affair where two families are brought together and establish a new bond and relationship, the local church is called upon to support the families at this crucial time. It is recommended that the local church exercises its pastoral care and counselling of the parties involved. It is also strongly recommended that the local pastor or his/her representative is present during betrothal and is available to pray with them.

2 Church weddings have become popular to some extent and the wedding eve and actual wedding day are very important not only to the couple getting married but also to the whole family. Representatives of the local church should be present during these moments. There may be need for a liturgy of special prayer at the moment the bride actually leaves home to go to church for the wedding.

3 We noted that there are many Christian young people who are satisfied with a customary wedding and do not want to come to church for their wedding. The main reason given is that church weddings are very expensive. But we wish to reiterate that it is the people themselves who make weddings expensive and not the church. The church will solemnize marriage if the following minimum requirements are met:

3.1 Presence of the bride and bridegroom
3.2 Two witnesses
3.3 A relative to give away the girl
3.4 A church minister to conduct the wedding.

The church does not mind the kind of robes or dress worn by the couple and expensive receptions are not necessary.

4.1 The wedding day in African culture, whether done in a customary way or celebrated in church, should be a very happy occasion. The 1662 liturgy despite its usefulness in the past has not given room for the joyful celebration of a wedding service. For instance, in many cultures women come escorting the bride singing joyfully but on reaching the doors of the church the joy is left there. Then follows a solemn liturgy where even the climax of pronouncing the couple husband and wife is observed with absolute silence. We would recommend that new African wedding liturgies reflect a joyful celebration from beginning to end, and that the climax be marked by ululations, dancing, clapping, drumming, etc. The liturgy may also include poems, meaningful responses, relevant litanies, and readings from relevant Bible passages, as, e.g. the Song of Solomon.

4.2 We recommend that in the new provincial wedding liturgies, the vows taken by the bride and bridegroom be worded in exactly the same manner thus reflecting equality of gender.

4.3 We recommend that the person selected to give away the girl be made to say words of willingness to give the girl away thus:

> 'I . . . and the members of our family and relatives have consented to give *N.* and *N.* in marriage in the name of God.'

We recommend that the minister requests the congregation to be supporting the couple about to be married.

4.4 Whereas we recognize that the ring is a universal symbol of marriage we would nevertheless encourage the use of other cultural symbols to signify marriage and commitment to one another.

4.5 Where the couple requests to be given Holy Communion provision should be made for a brief eucharistic service.

5 We recommend that the signing of the certificates and presentation be done before the congregation.

6 BLESSING OF CUSTOMARY MARRIAGES

We recommend that there be a special liturgy for couples who have been married customarily and now wish to have the blessing of the church. It should be understood that couples married customarily and recognized as married by the community, should be recognized as such by the church. The service therefore should be for the blessing of their marriage and family.

7 BLESSING OF A CIVIL MARRIAGE

We recommend that a special liturgy be formulated for cases where couples previously married in a civil court wish to have their marriages blessed in church.

8 WEDDING SERVICE STRUCTURE

We suggest the following structure (not mandatory)

8.1 *Preliminaries:* Prayers and sending the bride from home
8.2 *Weddings:* Introduction; the purpose of marriage
8.3 Promises
8.4 Handing over the bride to groom
8.5 Vows and rings
8.6 Joining the couple, pronouncing them married and ululations, drums, etc.
8.7 Sermon
8.8 Prayers/Eucharist
8.9 Signing of certificates and presentation
8.10 Blessing and recession

Issues Arising

(a) Giving away the bride or bridegroom should be treated as an option
(b) Prayers for bride or groom when leaving home for church should also be optional
(c) Solemnity and boredom should be a thing of the past. There should be innovative ways of making a marriage liturgy as joyful as possible.
(d) Is customary marriage complete in itself or does it necessarily require the sanctioning of the church?
(e) The marriage liturgy should provide for thanksgiving for couples who have been living together in love, albeit in customary marriage.
(f) We cannot really talk of Christian marriage but a marriage of Christians
(g) The marriage liturgy needs to give provision for remarriage of divorcees.

5. DEATH AND BURIAL LITURGY

The African Christian's attitude to death is inevitably shaped both by African tradition and the Christian belief. Some traditional beliefs can be, and have been, incorporated into Christian use; others must be subjected to criticism based on the gospel and the tradition of the Church. There are a number of issues that an African burial liturgy must address: they include the traditional difference in status between married and unmarried men, and women and children and the attitude to suicides and to criminals, time and place of burial, the mourning and memorial services, the distribution of possessions and the naming of children after the deceased.

Traditionally, Africans have tended to believe that death is not just natural but caused by some spirits or by other human beings, especially enemies, neighbours and relatives. In consequence, those who offer comfort to the bereaved need to remind them that, whatever the immediate cause of death, all life belongs to God; it is the Lord who gives and the Lord who takes away, and we are never separated from the love of Christ.

The Church is called to provide comfort and consolation to those who mourn, both strong and weak, Christians and non-Christian. There is also a need to prepare people for death and to help them to understand Christian teaching about it. The death of a Christian and the associated rites provide an occasion for the proclamation of the resurrection of Jesus Christ, and this should be central to the pastoral ministry of comfort.

In death, all encounter the God of judgment and of mercy, and it is not appropriate for the Church or individuals to exercise those rights that belong to God alone. All are to be commended to God's mercy. A particular difficulty may be found with those who have taken their own lives, but even here the Church commends them to the divine mercy, praying that they may be granted the forgiveness which Jesus came to bring.

GENERAL NOTES

1 The family of the deceased should have the various possibilities for the funeral liturgy explained and be allowed to choose what is most appropriate.
2 The practice in certain African societies, as in some Eastern churches, is to anoint the body with oil prior to burial. This sign of love may appropriately be done for Christians.
3 Funerals may be celebrated at any lawful time. On Sundays, however, priority is given to the worship of the church.
4 The funeral rite need not take place within a church building, but may be conducted wherever is convenient, whether indoors or outdoors.
5 Any traditional customs concerning the burial which are appropriate for a Christian may be followed. The use of a coffin is not compulsory. Where the place of burial is not consecrated or set apart for Christian burial, a prayer of blessing should be said over the grave before interment.
6 It is appropriate to provide prayers for different types of people covering differences in age, status in community, and cause of death.
7 A memorial service held some time after the funeral is important for African societies. Provision for such a service according to local custom is appropriate for Christians.

EXAMPLES OF PRAYERS

. . . **(a): A Prayer at sudden death** (composed by the group)

O Lord, before you brought us into this world, you knew us. You also knew the number of days this (man) (woman) would live, but you hid it from us for your own good purposes. What is sudden to us was known to you before it existed; help us to go over it in your strength and accept it the way it came to us so that your name continues to be glorified and your people sustained. In Jesus' name we pray. Amen.

. . . **(b): Prayer for a child** (from the Southern African Prayer Book)

Heavenly Father, your Son, our Saviour took little children into his arms and blessed them: receive your child N, in your never failing care and love comfort those who have loved (him) (her) on earth and bring us all to your everlasting kingdom; through Jesus Christ our Lord, who lives and reigns with you and the Holy Spirit, one God, now and for ever.

. . . **(c): Prayer for a single man or woman** (composed by the group)

Almighty God, your Son Jesus Christ commended the dignity of marriage and showed by his example, the value of the single life. he called both the single and the married to be his disciples. We thank you for the life of our brother N and ask you to receive him into the joy of your kingdom, where there will be neither marrying nor giving in marriage, but all the faithful will be united in your love, through Jesus Christ our Lord. Amen.

. . . **(d): Prayer for a suicide** (composed by the group)

Lord Jesus Christ, you knew the agony of the garden and the loneliness of the cross, but remained in the love of your Father. We commend N to your mercy and claiming no judgment for ourselves, commit him/her to you, the righteous judge of all, now and for ever. Amen.

. . . **(e): Prayer on the death of both parents** (composed by the group)

God Almighty, you are the head of all families on earth, we thank you for the lives of your servants N and N, for the good example they have been to their children and family. We ask you to help their children feel your presence with them always and in your tender love wipe away all tears from their eyes; through Christ our Lord. Amen.

Issues Arising

(a) Prayers about the dead could be put as an appendix for alternative selection.
(b) Prayers should not so much be directed towards the dead but to the bereaved family and community.
(c) The family should be given liberty to choose parts of the liturgy which best applies to them.
(d) The following are not absolutely necessary: a church service; a coffin.
(e) The liturgy traditionally has not provided for wailing and mourning or memorial service; but these are needed.
(f) After the burial service, then what? Do we just remove the robes and disappear?
(g) Necessary for inclusion—liturgy for sick people, liturgy for soul dismissal.

4. Beginning the Response: A Nigerian Contribution

by Solomon Amusan

Having studied with much pleasure the Report of the Kanamai Consultation as it deals with African culture and the Anglican forms of worship and its conflicts with the traditional culture of the people of Africa, I find with John Pobee that:

> 'No good purpose is served by proceeding to vitriolic attacks on the earliest missionaries . . . our task now is to build on where they left off, and remedy their errors.'[1]

The major part of this opening response covers the first ten pages of the Report, that is the Introduction to Section 2.6 and the Conclusion. Certainly, I want to start by saying that most of the points raised in sections 3-5e of the Report are similar to what is practised in Nigeria. It is then pointless to make an extended submission on these rather than simply to endorse them which I gladly do. One needs to appreciate the spirit of the participants that

> 'suggestions made in this report are not recommendations for implementation but are intended to raise questions and issues of importance.'[2]

Therefore in agreement with the Principles and Guidelines for Liturgical Renewal as proposed in the Report, the fundamental issue is to seek an alternative approach to form the basis of making the Anglican forms of worship relevant to the cultural setting of African Christians. This could perhaps lead to a new definition of the liturgy.[3] Since the Anglican Communion has no central liturgical text as the Roman Catholic Church does[4], such a definition would re-emphasize the purpose of worship in the contemporary rites. Not only would this strengthen the role of Christian society, it would also help the church to live as a family. Unless this is done, with all the Western influences that exist in Africa, Christian worship and Christian rites will continue to be regarded as alien institutions intruding upon, but not integrated with, social institutions.[5]

A contemporary African tends to see the traditional culture as being, even if in a highly rarefied sense, the 'African Old Testament' through which God has revealed himself to the people of that culture. Traditional religious practice is

---

[1] John Pobee, 'The Christian Church Attitude to Indigenous Beliefs'; paper presented at the Annual Conference of the West African Association of Theological Insitutions, 1979, p.2.

[2] Statement Section 2.1. See p.40 above.

[3] *Ibid.* Section 1.3 under 'Issues Arising' (b). See p.39. above.

[4] *Ibid.* Section 1.2. See p.38 above.

[5] Martin Jarret-Kerr, *Patterns of Christian Acceptance* (London, 1972) pp.65-76

then regarded as a reflection of that true universal religion. This is compatible with Oepke who argues that

> '. . . all positive religions are only reflections of a universal original religion and a type of Christianity, and Christianity is the antitype and prototype.'[1]

This was the view held by the church after the post-Constantinian revolution when Christianity became a public institution.[2] Thus, for instance, Gregory the Great, in his reply to Augustine of Canterbury's inquiry about which liturgical tradition should be introduced to Anglo-Saxon Christians, not only was tolerant of Christian ritual traditions differing from those he knew in Rome, but also instructed Augustine to accommodate them.[3]

Gregory regarded the old traditions of the English people before Christianity was introduced as at least potentially pointing forward to Christianity. This helped the propagation of the gospel. Inability on the part of Christian missions to take such a step in the last one hundred years, in recognizing African Culture as a type of their 'Old Testament', has led to conflicts of culture and consequently to the proliferation of separate churches, as we now witness in all African countries.

The struggle of the colonized countries aimed at human liberation, not only at the social, political and economic levels, but especially at the religious level of life.[4] Full liberation based on biblical teachings has a more comprehensive character than political liberation because it also involves spiritual freedom. This is why we now speak of indigenization, contextualization, inculturation and liberation of liturgy. It must be noted that 'missionary Christianity', as brought to Africa in general, developed its own appropriate theology—namely 'colonial theology', which has resulted in 'imperialistic theology'. Consequently we are now witnessing liturgical imperialism which implies imposition of foreign liturgy, thus discouraging the Africans from thinking about a concept of liturgical practice of their own. Liturgy and liturgical theology lack their full potential until they become deeply ingrained, virtually instinctive and natural expressions of faith and of the nature of God for the people who are actually worshipping. Admission of any form of indigenization, adaptation, inculturation of English liturgy in this century is an admission of the African liturgists of their failure to face the liturgical challenges; for they have been forgetting that the English liturgy, with its theology, as handed down by the missionaries, was shaped by the same community that later produced those who imposed imperial domination upon Africa. Until there is an appropriate African liturgical theology which will speak of a God who is as truly the God of the Africans as the God of any other continent, we cannot be really involved with Africans in the real sense, for the theology of English rite defends the structure of their concept and culture. An appropriate liturgical theology developed in the context of the

---

[1] A. Oekpe, *Das neue Gottesrolk* (1950) p.124 cited by H. Visser t' Hooft, *No other Names* (London, 1963) p.11.

[2] R. C. D. Jasper and Paul Bradshaw, *A Companion to the Alternative Service Book* (SPCK, London, 1986), pp.5 & 6.

[3] See E. Elochukwuu Uzukwu, *Truly Christian, Truly African* (Nairobi, 1982) p2.

[4] This is implied in the present struggle of the colonized countries for liturgical freedom.

African situation will help the churches in Africa, and does not *need* indigenization or adaptation or contextualization because it is enveloped within the African concept of God.

With regard to this, an African liturgical theology needs to be sought. This type of theology will become a helpful instrument instead of a hindrance in the struggle of the Africans. As the church of God, we must recognize the need to correct historical failures of the past and contemporary failings of the present, in order not to lose faithfulness to God and his love.

The English liturgical theology as imported into Africa does not unite active engagement with relevant analysis so as to overcome the liturgical 'crisis' as rightly observed by the Consultation.[1] To avoid either mere activism or escapist analysis, a new way has to be developed to forge a practical analysis out of the struggle to strip from the African Christians foreign liturgical cultures which have hitherto alienated them from true perception of Christianity; and to use that liturgical analysis in an ongoing concept for an African liturgical theology. This in turn should provide active engagement in the struggles for liberation with a corresponding new concept and form of liturgy in the contextual and theological dimensions.

At present, as rightly observed by the Consultation, various descriptions of liturgical change have also been adopted, to indicate the process of trying to de-imperialize liturgical theology and to avoid imitation of foreign practice currently held in African countries. Various terms are used, as e.g. 'indigenization', 'inculturation', 'incarnation'.[2] All these terms may still have some lurking elements of 'colonial and/or missionary theology'.

The need to de-imperialize Africans of the inherited English rite demands a search for a new liturgical theology, developing a fresh and contemporary concept and form rather than the English rites imposed on the church in Africa. From the origins of the presence of Christianity in Africa, we can say that it was not an authentic Christian liturgical practice which came to Africa,but a Christian liturgy which had already been indigenized in a highly peculiar way by the English culture and yet was brought to Africa as a kind of universalizable Christian liturgy.

Almost all that appears to have been done so far in the Anglican Churches in Africa is to translate the English Prayer Book into the vernacular, often forcing the vernacular into an English rhythm and idiom producing what Pobee describes as 'musical nonsense'[3], and thus creating what Idowu calls 'spiritual serenity'[4] and which, in Britain, would be a spiritual anaesthetic! This is not to criticize the integrity of the original missionary work but to contest the implication of that negative attitude by equating Christianity to the English way of life.

The mere fact that the English rite with its concepts is adopted by the Church of England does not make it automatically and authentically Christian or

[1] The general mood of the Consultation depicts the fact that there is a liturgical crisis in the Anglican Churches in Africa.

[2] The Report, Section 2.1. See p.39 above.

[3] John Pobee, *op. cit,* p.1.

[4] Bolaji Idowuu, *Towards An Indigenous Church* (London, 1965) p.8.

appropriate in other countries and cultures. Any concept or term adopted by the church requires constant checking and needs to be supported either in detail or spirit by reference to the historical sources of each term or practice or concept. This is an important point which we need to uphold before thinking of any structure as proposed in the Consultation report.[1] The African concept of the liturgy will lead to the form the structure has to follow.

This type of concept may eventually become the African Anglican Identity, in which the African church operates and thus becomes a legacy for the future generation and a contribution to the wider Anglican Communion.

[1] The Statement, Section 1.2: Examples No. 2 paragraph 2 and 3; and Section 1.3 under 'Steps for implementation'.

THE GROUP FOR RENEWAL OF WORSHIP (GROW)

This Group, originally founded in 1961, has for well over twenty years taken responsiblity for the Grove Books publications on liturgy and worship. Its membership and broad aims reflect a highly reforming, pastoral and missionary interest in worship. Beginning with a youthful evangelical Anglican membership in the early 1970s, the Group has not only probed venturously into the future Anglican worship, but has also with growing sureness of touch taken its place in promoting weighty scholarship. Thus the list of 'Grove Liturgical Studies' (available in the publisher's stock-list) shows how, over a twelve-year period, the quarterly Studies added steadily to the material available to students of patristic, reformation and modern scholarly issues in liturgy. In 1986 the Group was approached by the Alcuin Club Committee with a view to publishing the new series of Joint Liturgical Studies, and this series is, at the time of writing, in its eighth year of publication, sustaining the programme with three Studies each year.

Between the old Grove Liturgical Studies and the new Joint Liturgical Studies there is a large provision of both English language texts and other theological works on the patristic era. A detailed list is available from the publishers.

Since the early 1970s the Group has had Colin Buchanan as chairman and Trevor Lloyd as vice-chairman.

THE ALCUIN CLUB

The Alcuin Club exists to promote the study of Christian liturgy in general, and in particular the liturgies of the Anglican Communion. Since its foundation in 1897 it has published over 130 books and pamphlets. Members of the Club receive some publications of the current year free and others at a reduced rate.

Information concerning the annual subscription, applications for membership and lists of publications is obtainable from the Treasurer, The Revd. T. R. Barker, 11 Abbey Street, Chester CH1 2JF. (Tel. 0244 347811, Fax 0244 347823).

The Alcuin Club has a three-year arrangement with the Liturgical Press, Collegeville, whereby the old tradition of an annual Alcuin Club major scholarly study has been restored. The first title under this arrangement was published in early 1993: Alastair McGregor, *Fire and Light: The Symbolism of Fire and Light in the Holy Week Services.*

The Joint Liturgical Studies have been reduced to three per annum from 1992, and the Alcuin Club subscription now includes the annual publication (as above) and the three Joint Liturgical Studies. The full list of Joint Liturgical Studies follows overleaf. All titles are in print.

Alcuin/GROW Joint Liturgical Studies

All cost **£3.95 (US $8) in 1994**

1987 TITLES

1. **(LS 49) Daily and Weekly Worship—from Jewish to Christian** by Roger Beckwith, Warden of Latimer House, Oxford
2. **(LS 50) The Canons of Hippolytus** edited by Paul Bradshaw, Professor of Liturgics, University of Notre Dame
3. **(LS 51) Modern Anglican Ordination Rites** edited by Colin Buchanan, then Bishop of Aston
4. **(LS 52) Models of Liturgical Theology** by James Empereur, of the Jesuit School of Theology, Berkeley

1988 TITLES

5. **(LS 53) A Kingdom of Priests: Liturgical Formation of the Laity: The Brixen Essays** edited by Thomas Talley, Professor of Liturgics, General Theological Seminary, New York.
6. **(LS 54) The Bishop in Liturgy: an Anglican Study** edited by Colin Buchanan, then Bishop of Aston
7. **(LS 55) Inculturation: the Eucharist in Africa** by Phillip Tovey, research student, previously tutor in liturgy in Uganda
8. **(LS 56) Essays in Early Eastern Initiation** edited by Paul Bradshaw, Professor of Liturgics, University of Notre Dame

1989 TITLES

9. **(LS 57) The Liturgy of the Church in Jerusalem** by John Baldovin
10. **(LS 58) Adult Initiation** edited by Donald Withey
11. **(LS 59) 'The Missing Oblation': The Contents of the Early Antiochene Anaphora** by John Fenwick
12. **(LS 60) Calvin and Bullinger on the Lord's Supper** by Paul Rorem

1990 TITLES

13-14 **(LS 61) The Liturgical Portions of The Apostolic Constitutions: A Text for Students** edited by W. Jardine Grisbrooke (This double-size volume, costs double price (i.e. £7.90 in 1994)).

15. **(LS 62) Liturgical Inculturation in the Anglican Communion** edited by David Holeton, Professor of Liturgics, Trinity College, Toronto
16. **(LS 63) Cremation Today and Tomorrow** by Douglas Davies, University of Nottingham

1991 TITLES

17. **(LS64) The Preaching Service—The Glory of the Methodists** by Adrian Burdon, Methodist Minister in Rochdale
18. **(LS65) Irenaeus of Lyon on Baptism and Eucharist** edited with Introduction, Translation and Commentary by David Power, Washington, D.C.
19. **(LS66) Testamentum Domini** edited by Grant Sperry-White, Department of Theology, Notre Dame
20. **(LS67) The Origins of the Roman Rite** Edited by Gordon Jeanes, Lecturer in Liturgy, University of Durham

1992 TITLES

21. **The Anglican Eucharist in New Zealand 1814-1989** by Bosco Peters, Christchurch, New Zealand

22-23. **Foundations of Christian Music: The Music of Pre-Constantinian Christianity** by Edward Foley, Capuchin Franciscan, Chicago (second double-sized volume at £7.90 in 1994))

1993 TITLES

24. **Liturgical Presidency** by Paul James
25. **The Sacramentary of Sarapion of Thmuis: A Text for Students** edited by Ric Barrett-Lennard, West Australia
26. **Communion Outside the Eucharist** by Phillip Tovey, Banbury, Oxon.

1994 TITLES

27. **Revising the Eucharist: Groundwork for the Anglican Communion** edited by David Holeton, Dean of Trinity College, Toronto
28. **Anglican Liturgical Inculturation in Africa** edited by David Gitari, Bishop of Kirinyaga, Kenya (June 1994)

29-30. **On Baptismal Fonts: Ancient and Modern** by S. Anita Stauffer, Lutheran World Federation, Geneva (September, 1994) (Double-sized volume at £7.90)